Delight Your Husband:

The Christian Wife's Manual to

Passion, Confidence & Oral Sex

Belah Rose

Preface

Are you ready for incredible transformation and freedom in your intimacy? Do you desire to see that twinkle in his eye and excitement on his face when he sees you enter the room? Is there a pull on your heart to really get this "intimacy thing" finally figured out?

I've been in your shoes and by God's grace, I'm now on the other side and want to help you on this path. I'm proud of you. It takes courage to move towards wholeness, healing and sexual freedom.

Since publishing Delight Your Husband in 2014 and beginning the Delight Your Marriage podcast in 2015, I have been amazed at the global impact of this work.

I always knew God had a lot more to say about intimacy and His people needed to be empowered by the truth ALONG WITH practical tools to have incredible sexual passion in their marriages.

But more than that, I knew that if His people were able to move forward with the principles of generous love making, they would become "one flesh" in a way that fuels their Kingdom work and aligns them with God's will.

By God's grace, that is what I've seen over and over again.

As you read this book, I want to challenge you--the same way I challenge my clients--to have an open mind and a soft heart.

This isn't an easy topic. Maybe there will be dramatic enlightening aspects and parts of this book that make you squirm, and that's ok. Keep going and see what God might want you to see about that topic that you may not have before. Or maybe that piece has value for someone else's situation and not for your own. Or maybe it's just dead wrong, but the next few pages are "right on" and God needs you to see those things.

Is this a difficult topic? Yes. Is it going to take effort to revisit some of your past understandings, humbly look at your opinions, and maybe even difficult experiences to get to the other side for joy and relaxation in intimacy? Yes.

But if you've been married any length of time, you know that this topic is a vital one. And one that just about no one is willing to talk about. Especially in a scripture-based way.

The contents that follow have been used by sex therapists in working with their clients. Women who have experienced horrific sexual trauma specifically around oral sex have been able to breakfree from their past. Marriage therapists and licensed social workers have been shocked at the level of insights of its specificity and guidance.

I am so grateful that God has used the pages that follow to transform women's lives and their hearts. The significant impact on their husbands. Then the ripple effect on their kids, ministries, work-life and with whom all those you interact. They have emailed their stories. I hope you will too: belah@delightyourmarriage.com

They get to a level of freedom like they never have had before. But then some seek more. They realize they've come a long way, but they want to gain more tools, encouragement and even accountability to have every kind of intimacy: emotional, spiritual and physical. So, like them, you now have access to the Delight Your Husband FREE resources at www.delightyourhusband.com/bonuses

And some want the whole package. She wants to become the fiery seductress, a woman who enjoys spiritual sexuality, knows how to become a woman cherished and get her desires met in and out of the bedroom. These women join one of my team coaching programs to gain access to my proven system and work directly with me on its implementation in their lives.

It's the recipe that by God's grace therapists who work with wives have gone through and transformed their own marriages and how they serve their clients. I've worked with marriage leaders whose own marriages needed help and the program has "changed their marriage!" This step-by-step program has even been used for those on the brink of divorce--where the husband was still having an affair--and now they're the best they've ever been. He's saying "I love you more than anything". All this within a couple of months.

If you're ready for these kind of life transformations and tailored guidance, proven recipe and renewed passion, butterflies-in-your-stomach results, you can learn more at delightyourhusband.com/recipe

You are taking a huge step by diving into this book. I am so excited for you and the resulting changes in your marriage, family, joy, peace, and ultimately your walk with God. This can change everything.

Some of the many comments from my clients:

- Tracey
  - On the edge of divorce after her husband had an affair. They had a young daughter and she was desperate to save her marriage.
  - Would you recommend others working with Belah and why?
    - YES, 100% YES! Belah gave me a new perspective on sex, my husband, my marriage, my relationship with God and view of myself.
    - I am forever grateful for her saving me and my marriage. We were on the brink of divorce...when I asked my husband about me working with Belah, he said "Might as well – if it doesn't work, you will be able to say we tried everything."
    - Now: "We are the happiest we've been since the first few months of marriage"
- Vallerie
  - She never had ANY physical desire for sex and felt interest in sex was sinful. She also felt pressured because she felt he had expectations of her.
  - Now: She feels free and her body CRAVES sex!!
  - Would you recommend this program? To whom? Why?
    - TO EVERYONE!! I would recommend this program to couples struggling in their marriage, as well as couples who have wonderful marriages (like mine)

who would like to enhance their lives in a real way! I think Bella can turn around marriages with her program and improve successful marriages in a big way

- Shannon
    - She's a therapist, but their relationship was really tough—living as roommates. He'd stay late at work, on the weekends ignore her while watching football, and let her handle parenting on her own.
    - Now: He's active in his kids' lives, he comes home early from work, does a ton of stuff around the house without being asked—oh and they have amazing sex!
    - What difference has Belah made in your life?
        - I cannot express the difference that this makes in my life. What is different? EVERYTHING.
- Jessica
    - Before working with Belah, my marriage had been to the brink of divorce and separation. My husband and I had continual anger and resentment toward one another. I knew the importance of sex to a man, and felt pressure to be 'enough'. But I felt like I never was.
    - I reached out to Belah, for her to help me be who he needed. Belah listened to my heart, and saw the missing piece- boundaries. Turns out, he needed ME all along.
    - Through Belah's coaching, she helped me with: Healthy boundaries. Loving and respecting myself. Realizing, and honoring what "I" enjoy and desire about sex and intimacy. She gave me wisdom and words to say. Teaching me what a healthy relationship looks like in all areas.
    - The amazing benefits I am enjoying now: LOVE; true love like never before. My husband and I look forward to being around each other, and have such an appreciation and respect for one another. I am cherished and honored, he is respected and lifted up as my man. I am more "me"

than ever before, and loving exactly who I am and am becoming.
- ○ Through working with Belah, my marriage is saved and thriving, and I am forever changed and grateful.

I'm excited to add your story to the list! Also, don't forget to get access to the FREE private bonuses: delightyourhusband.com/bonuses

May you be blessed and empowered through this journey!

Love,

Belah

For my darling husband. You are my daily delight.

--

2nd Edition:
The many men and women who listen and follow this ministry, may this book be a support to your life and the ripples impact everything you touch.

Delight Your Husband
Table of Contents

Section I

Introduction

Introduction

Want to Grab a Coffee?

I love coffee shops. I sit in one almost every day, either writing, working, or chatting with a dear friend. Something about the hustle and bustle of people ordering their morning joe, clanging dishes, laughing about their day, and the smell of freshly brewed lattes, makes me feel energized and comfortable. My favorite thing to do in a coffee shop is sit with a close friend and pour out our lives to each other while sipping our mugs.

That is how I think about this book. The topic is not one that should be posted on billboards or spoken from pulpits. If I could sit across from you at a coffee shop, if we could share our lives together, that would be my preference. After years of friendship; we'd laugh, cry, get red in the face, congratulate one another on the new life milestone, compliment and encourage each other, apologize for thoughtless comments, and we'd be uncomfortably transparent. Eventually, we'd have come to a place where the topic of intimacy in marriage floated to the top. You could share your struggles and I could relate. I could offer the years of pain and learning I have gone through and come to a place of peace and new discovery.

Maybe your marriage is at a good place and you desire for deeper physical intimacy and I could share specific how-tos. Maybe you're uncomfortable with areas of the marriage bed and I could help guide you to a place where God has shown my heart a greater purpose and freedom. Maybe you are in a place of brokenness and desperation in the area of intimacy and truly need hope in this area. I have been there. I want to know your story. I want to know where you are in your journey. I want to know what has brought you to a place of wanting a deeper sexual connection with your husband. I want to share about my journey and practical keys that have been invaluable to me. Wherever you are, I pray this course will be a source of light and hope for you as you reimagine what your marriage could be, and work towards that vision.

Talking About Sex

I took a moment to reflect, recently, and realized there are many challenging areas of life that are not discussed openly. In these areas the people struggling have no way of getting better because it is not addressed head-on. Sex is in this category. The topic of this book is sex and the practicalities of peni in marriage (I'll talk about what that means in a minute). If you knew me in my home life, professional life, and church life, you probably wouldn't dream that I would write a book about the marital passion and practicalities of peni. To reiterate, I do not think this topic should be discussed publicly. It is a private area of your heart and marriage. It deserves delicate and careful handling. The problem is many Christian women are suffering in silence. Suffering with insecurities and questions without any outlet, because we do not discuss "such things". But, the Bible takes a different tone. In Titus 2:3-4 "Older women...*train the young women to love their husbands...*" Among other things, the women who have a level of understanding in loving their husbands are *supposed* to teach those who do not. That is not a culture I see in the church and yet it is a *great* need. Though I cannot sit across a coffee table and chat about these intimate topics, I aim to provide that understanding and support through these pages.

What Is This Course About?

This course is about moving out of pain and into peace, even pleasure. I have been through too much hardship around the topic of sex to not help my sisters who struggle in the same way.

This course is about God's kindness and how He gently led me from utter brokenness and hurt to a place of wholeness and confidence in my sexuality. I grew up thinking the sex-act was dirty and that my body and vulnerability was not desirable. I have now uncovered and share in these pages God's truth about how He sees sex, our body, and our vulnerable hearts.

This course bridges the gap for the wife who wants to be a holy daughter of God and a sensual lover to her husband. There are many heart issues that come into play around sexual intimacy. Many perspectives, experiences, and misguided teachings that get in the way of women achieving wholeness and freedom in this area. A woman must look deep inside herself to understand the things inhibiting her and how to move past them. This course will ask you tough questions that need to be wrestled with in order to come out victorious.

This course is about oral sex, but uses the word "peni", short for penilingus (aka felatio). This new word should just be associated with the intimate exchange between you and your husband. I find that all the other synonyms conjure up images of sin or possibly inappropriate subject matter. Instead, use this new word to conjure up images of just you and your husband enjoying each other and loving this act together.

This course is about the how-tos of peni. There were plenty of things in the bedroom I heard about but didn't know how to do. However, Christian books didn't give enough practical, step-by-step information. Generally, I was told "if you're comfortable with it, go for it". But that didn't help me *get comfortable* because I didn't know *what* to do or what God thought about it. This book gives you the clarity to actually understand how your husband works and how you can bring your husband to amazing sexual fulfillment. I focus specifically on peni because I think many women are hung up in this area. Yet if they could master this part of intimacy, they would have a foundational understanding giving them the confidence to discover all other areas. This book shares with you biblical, scientific, and experiential wisdom on this topic. Each area is vital for becoming a free, godly, and generous lover.

After engaging in this course, you will have the confidence and practicalities to approach your husband confidently. This course is about pleasuring your husband. It is focused on what *you* can do in the bedroom to create a fulfilling, intimate marriage for both of you. You will understand how his orgasm works. You will understand his libido, erections, attitude, necessities, and I give solutions to specific challenges surrounding the act.

As you read and engage, you may notice some repetition of central themes. I do this to make sure you *get* these vital pieces. Repetition is a key to memory. If there are topics you notice are reiterated in different ways throughout this course, try to internalize these points so they will stay with you long after you are finished with this course.

How This Course Is Set Up

Book -

There are four major sections of the book: Love the Act, Love Yourself, Love Your Husband, and Love His Member. To get to a place of freedom and confidence in the bedroom, there is quite a lot of wrong thinking that needs to be corrected. In Love the Act, we will go through the areas that may be blocking your sex life from being fully enjoyable, including fears, God's view, body image, and God's ultimate purposes of sex in marriage. In Love Yourself, we will explore how to be sexually whole, reconnect to your body, and awaken your sexual desires. In Love Your Husband, we will talk about how he thinks and his desires for sex as different than our own. We discuss the importance of understanding how he works in order to love him best. Lastly, Love His Member is a much more practical and step-by-step walkthrough of peni. For married eyes only--this section will get into the nitty-gritty of pleasuring your hubby below the belt. I give very specific and usable information so that you walk away from this course knowing exactly what to do in your next steamy encounter.

Notes from Ms. Susan -

After writing this book, I interviewed an amazing woman who has been married for 30 years to the same man, has a couple of biological kids (and *many* other spiritual ones). She has had some incredible highs and serious challenges throughout her journey. She also has a Masters in Pastoral Counseling and has led pre-marital counseling for over 15 years. She has observed and walked with couples in marriages at every extreme: beginning, vibrant, stagnating, and--sadly--tearing apart. She loves her husband and God's plan for marriage. It is one of the best marriages I have ever seen. She is so generous to give us advice in many areas touched on throughout this book. Let her words impact you deeply as they come from a depth of experience and lived-out wisdom.

Steamy To Dos -

I realize this is a journey for you my sister, and all of us. It is not going to be automatic or instantaneous to move from the "usual" to the "spicy and spontaneous". Give yourself time to think through, write about, and process what is offered here. I also want to get you used to taking some small risks with your husband at every stage of this process. I want to get you out of your comfort zone little by little and try new things and new ways of interacting. In the Steamy To-Dos section, I include some items to try with your husband as you're going through this book. They start off fairly tame, but as you increase in understanding and confidence, you'll have more adventurous Steamy To Dos. If you do them (as uncomfortable as they may feel in the beginning), you'll slowly get to a place where it feels more natural. But that feeling will not come without your action. An imperfect action is *always* better than a perfect plan, never done.

Workbook/Journal -

Did you know we learn best when we articulate our own thoughts? That is why the best teachers ask you questions instead of lecturing all class long. Think of the last time you were able to truly share your heart with a good friend. Did you come away feeling glad for the things you uncovered about yourself while you were just speaking? It is probably because until you moved from passing thoughts to putting them into words, you weren't totally aware of how you felt. It is the same with the sexual journey. We are very unclear about our own thoughts, past, and feelings until we take the time and energy to put them into words. I ask you to do that in the Workbook. Throughout the book, I give specific areas and I ask for your *written* response.

This course is truly about life change. Ever notice how two people can read the same book and for one it totally revolutionizes her life, and the other simply moves on, unchanged? I want you to engage and go through the hard emotional work, so you leave this course very different than when you went into it. You have already invested the time to read through this introduction and the money to purchase. Both, you could have used on other things. But, I know you want a lasting change in your love-life. That is what the Workbook is for.

Go through the book and when I ask you to "write in your Workbook", stop. Be disciplined and answer it fully. Be curious about what is truly going on in your own heart as you read that chapter. Yes, it will take longer (maybe 4 times as long). But your marriage and your heart are worth it. How long are you going to struggle in the same pain when you have time and opportunity *now* to accomplish true freedom? I truly believe that your level of engagement in the Workbook *will determine* your level of results through this course. Please, do not skip these; it is so vital in order to have the marriage you ultimately want. There will be so many "Aha!" moments as you dig deep into *your* opinions and responses to what is offered here in your Workbook.

On a practical side, you can print out the separate PDF Workbook to write in separately. Or to be more environmentally-friendly, (my preference!) for this course, I have inserted the questions also in the Book so you may write the answers in your own journal as you are reading. This way you also can write without having to flip back and forth on your screen. (If you purchased the printed , the workbook is not printed separately.)

Why Should You Focus On Sex?

In the midst of so much difficulty and hardship in the world, this topic is *completely* worth your focus. A healthy, loving, and passionate marriage supports *every* other part of your life and your walk with God. I also found an unfulfilling marriage negatively affects *every* part of your life. It is a drain on your energy, emotions, and purposes. Sex is powerful and, with God's help, can transform your marriage. Once a woman understands and has confidence in bringing her husband to a fantastic orgasm in peni, she has all the tools needed to learn to pleasure him in every other way for the rest of their lives together. Spend the time mastering this part of life and it will serve both of you exponentially in your support and love for each other, every day thereafter. I am a big believer in focusing on one aspect of life until it is mastered before moving to the next. This is a vital area that deserves your attention because once you get it, you'll be able to move to many more amazing things with God and your husband.

Are You Ready?

Jesus said truth, like seed, can fall along fertile soil and grow into mighty trees. But other seeds along the path, rocks, and shallow soil--will never take root or realize their potential (Mark 4:1-20). How is your heart? Are you on fertile soil? Are you ready for God's truth to transform you in a way to take your marriage to amazing heights? Take a moment and ask God to ready your heart to understand, to receive, to process, and to be changed by His truth I aim to elucidate in this program. Pray with me: *Lord, I thank you for bringing me to this point of desire for change in my marital intimacy. I ask you to prepare my heart to receive your truth and help me to discern how to apply it to my life. Help me to see where and how you want me to heal and change in the area of sex. I love you. Thank you for being on this journey with me and helping me every step of the way.*

My Real Self, A Different Name

Belah Rose is not my real name. As I shared before, I desire a trusting friendship between you and I. We, ladies, cannot discuss such intimate topics without a significant level of trust. As I bare my soul, my experience, and what I've learned, I hope that gives you courage to "go there" in your own heart (and write it in your Workbook) as well. I hope it helps you go into your past, into your pain, and reflect; to ask God to come in and heal those deep areas. I want you to feel encouraged to go to those intimate, difficult areas and let the His light in. I will model that vulnerability throughout my writing in this book.

However, I would normally only be so vulnerable with my closest friends, as I feel that is what is appropriate and Biblical. I very much agree with Proverbs 4:18 which says "Guard your heart, above all else, for everything you do flows from it." I want to help more women than I can coach one-on-one and spend years developing this trusting bond before divulging. I want to give that level of trust and understanding to you while protecting my own heart and family. For this reason, I have chosen to write under a pen name, "Belah Rose" and I refer to my husband as "D".

I truly believe as women of God, we are to meditate on "whatever is true, whatever is noble, whatever is right, whatever is pure, whatever is lovely, whatever is admirable--if anything is excellent or praiseworthy--think on these things" (Philippians 4:8). In this book I aim to align with this scripture. Your sexual life in marriage is pure, lovely, and noble. I will clarify how and why in the following pages. However, I also agree that we are to keep our marital intimacy private. This book is not a call to indiscrete disclosure, it is a call to living out the verse: "older women...train the young women to love their husbands..." (Titus 2:3-4). I want to help women in areas that have been neglected by the older women in their lives who should have helped and guided them through these struggles.

God Made Us Unique

God created sex and He made men and women differently. On top of that, He made each man and each woman unique. There are specific things that each of us find particularly sexually pleasurable and others that are not. We each have unique erogenous zones. As women, we are wired very differently than men. In this book, I intend to elucidate many of those general differences. But as a wife, your job is to find out the peculiarities of *your* husband. Though I will outline many areas of the male mind and body that are generally universal, it would not be fair to assume your husband will fit into every category.

I'm sure you'd appreciate your husband reading a book on pleasing his wife. But, I bet you wouldn't appreciate him assuming everything written is true of your body and personal preferences without checking with you. Be open to the facts generally, but also recognize your husband is an individual who you are getting to know. As you learn what is true of many men, you should put on your sleuth hat, and find out if it is also true of your husband. Feel free to try out new things with him, but be very receptive and interrogative for feedback. If something is quite out of the ordinary, it may be best to ask beforehand. Part of this journey is figuring out who *he* is and how he can best receive pleasure.

What is your goal?

Though we probably haven't met yet, I know one thing about you. You are a woman with guts. To purchase a course on such a steamy topic, how can you not be? For every woman who picks this up, there are 1000 others whose marriages need it. I am proud of you for taking this first step. You care about learning to love your husband in the ways he most appreciates. You care about and desire to delight your husband. I can tell you desire a vital and thriving marriage with your husband.

Have you thought about what your dream marriage would look like? If you imagined your marriage 30 years from now, how do you want your sexual intimacy to look? A very frank writer, Larry Winget, said "Nobody ever wrote down a plan to be broke, fat, lazy, or stupid. Those things are what happen when you don't have a plan". But that will not be you, my sister. You will set a course toward which the rest of this book (and your subsequent years) of marriage can be set upon. Take a moment and imagine the marriage you want, the passion you want to share, how you want to be as a sexually confident wife, and how you would like your husband to be towards you. Think about specifically how you'd like things to be in the marriage bed.

Write this goal in your Workbook #1. Be creative and specific, for example: "In 30 years, I want to have a playful, intimate, friendly, and passionate marriage. I want to be strong, healthy, and totally content with my body. I want my husband to be enraptured by my looks, my heart, and my character. I want our marriage bed to be an incredible place of passion and fun. A place where I feel free and know him better than he knows himself. I want to bring him more pleasure, intimately, than he even knew possible. I want to be surprising and energetic in our frequent intimate encounters. I want to be enjoyed, cherished, and brought to orgasm by my confident and patient husband." Feel free to let your imagination create an incredible future for your lives together. I'll pause so you can do that now.

If you haven't done so, write your goal now. If you don't have the time right now to devote to the most important human relationship in your life, then I would strongly encourage you to stop this program until you can really make it a priority. If writing a short paragraph is too much time or effort now, then, with my blessing, please go and do the thing that is on your mind. And then come on back so you can fully engage in this course to the benefit of your whole life!

Great job! I am proud you took the time to outline your 30-year intention. Honestly, most people don't articulate this vision. *And* most people don't achieve a dream marriage. As we continue on in this journey, I'm going to ask you to dig down a little deeper. I am asking you to let down your guard a bit. Let yourself explore some of your own fears, pains, mistakes, and areas needing healing and growth. Each of us have all of these, you are not alone dear sister. I pray that God would soften your heart and help you to realize that He loves you and He is willing to forgive *any* thing in your past (even from yesterday).

He wants you to recognize where you have made mistakes, so He can help you move towards repentance, forgiveness, and a deeper walk with Him. So often, I think we try to avoid regret--all the "should haves"--because we don't want to be in that pain. Many times that is the best route. Sometimes, however, God wants us to revisit some areas, because they are still affecting us. We may need to recall them to mind and process them so He can heal us and teach us valuable lessons, vital to our walk today. I may ask you to go to areas that are a little uncomfortable with the purpose of growth into the woman He desires you to become.

My Goal: Your Success

My goal is a more fulfilling marriage for you. Marriage is truly a funny thing. It touches every part of our lives. Our partner is the one human with whom we should be able to be completely vulnerable and enjoy deepest intimacy and love. Vulnerability is scary, no doubt about it. It's scary to open yourself completely to another person. What it requires is deep honesty. As you open up and allow honesty to give you freedom with your spouse, it provides room for God to change you and make you more like Himself. It provides a space for your husband to love you and be an avenue of God's love and grace. When I was dating D, I remember talking to dear friend about how deeply D's love was affecting me, bringing me even to tears. She encouraged me that God was healing my hurt through D's love. Looking back on those difficult experiences where I let myself be bare (emotionally) in front of him, I received a lot of God's healing for my past. I want you to have a wonderful marriage. Sure, you're not the only one responsible for it, but you have the power to do *a lot.*

Being Served In the Bedroom

Many women are much more comfortable serving than being served. Such women, like Martha (in the story of Martha and Mary in Luke 10:38-42), will read this book and be excited to have another tool in their toolbox to *serve*. I'm grateful for that heart and it is indeed the purpose of this book. I want to also encourage you to assess your marriage and possibly your next steps after this course. To be clear, *you* deserve to be served as well. Your marriage is not just about him. It is both of you entering into generous love for each other. My aim is to give you the tools to serve and truly delight your husband. Afterwards, only you can assess if you are not receiving the "serving" you deserve in your marriage and working on that vital area.

If you are in a rocky spot maritally, I would suggest you fully apply the keys learned here. Then, provide time in your marriage for healing and unifying (it may be a season where you're doing most of the serving). Then, when your marriage and intimacy is in a *much* better spot, bring up your concerns (using the Bedroom Talk Laws you'll learn).

Your marriage is not all about his pleasure; that is not what scripture indicates. "Husbands, love your wives, just as Christ loved the church and gave himself up for her" (Eph 5:25). Though this is the biblical standard, it may not be the reality of your marriage. Remember, though, you can only change you. I'd encourage you to do what you can on your part to invest into the health and "love bank" of your marriage. When your "love bank" reserves are high, you may be at a place that you can say something. Modelling generosity (without strings attached or resentment) in the bedroom will speak volumes to your spouse. He will feel so loved that he may be eager to pleasure you better. At the very least, after this course, he will be at a place to be much more receptive to the conversation.

A Note On Honesty

Beloved reader, thank you for engaging in this course. Please consider who else in your life would benefit from this material. I ask that you would send them the link: www.delightyourhusband.com and allow them to get the material online. Would you not send the material to anyone without their purchase? I trust that would abide by your conscience. Thank you so much for your honesty and your help in this!

Why Do This Program Now?

I want you to have a fantastic marriage so you can do what God has called you to do in your life. I do not want you to make sex an idol. It is not the most important goal in your life. No, it is a gift and a life-support for everything else. Spend some weeks and months focusing on this aspect. Get to a place of confidence so your lives together can be supported by this skill and mindset. I am praying for you as you embark on this journey. May God speak truth in your heart and help you to discern His ways.

The truth is if you do not make time now, you may never make the time. We either prioritize what is important in our lives now, or we often never get around to it. Review your 30 year goals, it is time to work towards them *today*. For the health and future of your family, marriage, and the rest of your life: grab a cup of coffee, sister, and let's dive in!

Section II

Love The Act

A Way Forward

What is Your Marriage Status Quo?

Does the status quo of your marriage feel less than enjoyable? Does the marriage bed feel downright painful (emotionally and/or physically)? I wrote this book because sex is an amazing opportunity for growth and healing in a marriage. Your marriage bed may be wrought with rejection, feelings of inadequacy, sadness, and even humiliation. I have experienced painful times. I remember putting myself "out there" just to be shut down. I want you to know that you are not alone. The statistics are truly frightening. "Roughly 46 percent of more recently married couples fail to reach their 25th wedding anniversary" [1]. The top five reasons for divorce vary from survey to survey. But generally, the first reason for divorce is financial problems and not far behind is sex problems [2]. Interestingly enough, a study found that increasing sexual intercourse from once a month to once a week would have the same mood-boosting effects as adding $50,000 a year in income [3]. Why not kill two birds with one stone? *A lot* can be attributed to the bedroom. If you're not satisfied with how things are in your marriage, investing in your sexual relationship is a great place to start.

How Pain Affects Everything

The enemy tells us when we're in pain "there is no hope". It's like we're work horses bound by all the harnesses and ropes of pain. Have you seen those horses on the streets with blinders to make them focus only on the road ahead and nothing in the periphery? In pain, we're just like them. We're moving forward with blinders on. We don't see who's around us wanting to help us. We don't even see who we're stepping on and hurting while in the struggle. We certainly don't see the help God wants to give us. We're believing that "He must not care or we wouldn't be in this mess". This is a lie.

God deeply cares about your situation. He cares about your heart. He cares about how you feel. He deeply cares about your marriage. I believe you are not reading this book by accident. The Bible says that "With the Lord, a day is like a thousand years, and a thousand years are like a day" (2 Pet 3:8). Think of it. He spends "months" in each moment of your life and He knows your heart, thoughts, and desires incredibly well. He knows your past and how you were wronged. He knows every tear you've cried even when no one else does. He knows your fears and insecurities. He cares about you deeply. I want you to feel these truths, dear reader. He wants you to throw off the blinders and shackles. He wants you to walk with your head held high in His light of freedom and victory. To get there, we need to evaluate where we are now. We need to look at our situation fully and take time to consider.

How Did You Get Here?

I am only a fan of talking about something that is painful if it leads to a better outcome. Sometimes, venting is helpful to heal. But frequently, women (myself included) spend far too much time in the 'venting' phase. Pontificating on how we've been wronged just takes us deeper into self-pity and despair. I want you to figure out where you are now, so that you can move *from* there. Author and speaker, Anthony Robbins, says that we're motivated by either pain or pleasure. There's no point wallowing in pain unless it moves you to action and gets you to greater pleasure. Be aware that I only want you to go into a place of pain because I think it is necessary for you to have a true sense of how to move forward. When you can identify the points of your past that are painful, then you can take steps to change them. If you're avoiding looking at the pain to try not to feel it, it is still there. It's like a sickness, growing whether you are admitting to it or not. The first step in change is awareness.

Write in your Workbook #2. Would you take a moment and write in your workbook the answer to the following questions:

1) What does your marriage feel like right now?

2) On a scale from 1-10 (10- being sensual, open, and delightful & 1- being horrible, sad, and awful) what is your honest rating of your marital intimacy?

3) Take a little time and think back about some pivotal points in your marriage. I bet there wasn't just one thing, but multiple experiences that have produced the current state of affairs. Would you jot down some notes on events that have moved you to this place?

It Can Change

I bet you have a pretty good picture as to where you are now in your marriage. For those of you who are anywhere below a 6, I want to speak to you. I am not content with things staying the way they are. I don't think you are either. We live this life once and it 'ain't no dress rehearsal'. Your marriage should be a sacred place of intimacy, healing from the battles of the world, and deep joy. Glance back up to your goals in your workbook. Do not give up hope. God wants to transform your marriage into what are the desires of your heart. He is for you and for your marriage. You have gone this far into the program because you had an inkling there are still things you can do to get your marriage back on track. You believe, deep down, that you can play a powerful part in God turning your marriage around. He wants to use you in this mission.

He wants to use you to change your husband's heart back towards you, this marriage, and ultimately to Him. He cares about your marriage. A good marriage draws you both closer to God. Just about any marriage (even one moving through a difficult season) can make you more like Jesus: teaching you in very practical ways to turn the other cheek, be a servant, walk in love, and be clothed in humility. No matter where we find ourselves, God is teaching us to be more like Him, if we follow His lead. Yes, even in the area of sex.

God can redeem your relationship. I have seen Him do it in many others' lives and my own. He has taken me and my marriage out of the slums of sin, pain, and brokenness and He has brought it to a place of healing, redemption, and deep love. *He* did this. But, He required me to be part of the solution. If we sit on the sidelines and wait to see God move, we're missing a great part of His plan. In His infinite wisdom, He has chosen *you* to play a vital role in your husband's life. He wants you to love your husband just as He loved you. He loved you so much that He gave His own life, so that we could know Him and be with Him.

Moving Forward

I want to be very clear about the way forward. Below are steps A, B, C, and D to give a sense of how we will move forward.

A-Acknowledge. Firstly, we've accomplished this. You have acknowledged your pain, where you are, and how you got there.

B-Pray. Secondly, acknowledge your need for God's help and ask fervently for it. For the rest of this course, pray daily for your husband and for your marriage. Set a reminder in your phone or calendar to pray every day for your marriage. As a starting place, pray: *God, I thank you for loving me so deeply and truly. Thank you for entrusting me with this marriage. I don't fully understand your plan, but God, I ask you to lead me and help me to be like Jesus in this marriage. Help me to love and serve my husband as deeply as You love me. Amen.* Please add to this prayer according to your story and where your marriage is.

C-Trust. Trust that God can move and believe that He is directing your path. "Trust in the LORD with all your heart and lean not on your own understanding; in all your ways submit to him, and he will make your paths straight." (Prov 3:5-6). When you begin to realize just how *big* God is and that He wants you to have a fulfilling marriage, your faith starts to shift. You start to see the bigger picture. Your goals don't seem silly or far-fetched; they're God-given dreams.

D-Learn and Act. Through this material and others, I ask you to apply your heart to wisdom and understanding. "Do not forsake wisdom, and she will protect you; love her, and she will watch over you" (Prov 4:6). Do your part. Learn all you can. Find out the dynamics of you and your husband. Determine the cycles and patterns you fall into. Recognize the areas *you* can change. Also recognize the areas you cannot change. You cannot change him; but you are a powerful 50% of your marriage. Do the hard work of recognizing your reactions and the buttons you push. Realize the ways *you* disengage, are guarded, and other areas in you God wants to mature you. Put the magnifying glass on yourself and figure out how you can be of use to God. "First take the plank out of your own eye, and then you will see clearly to remove the speck from your brother's eye" (Matt 7:5). Act daily to move your marriage in the right direction.

Action in the Bedroom

God has kindly given us many avenues to love one another. In The Five Love Languages book, Gary D. Chapman describes the many ways each of us experience love. He says we all experience love through five avenues: giving gifts, spending time together, affirming each other with words, physically touching, and doing acts of service for each other. Each of us have a specific way that is most enjoyable to us. Usually, one is more primary than the others of how we enjoy receiving and giving love. Further, men and women have more general ways that are specific to male and female. Lovemaking encompasses all of these languages. You can compliment each other, spend time, give/serve the other, and obviously there's quite a lot of physical touch.

One vital difference between many males and females is the importance of sex in showing love to one another. Generally, women experience sex as an opportunity for affection and physical closeness to their partners. But the male experience when in a committed relationship, is actually emotional closeness. A woman enjoys her orgasm, the tender touch of her husband, and serving her partner, but it is not *always* a source of emotional closeness. A woman may feel more loved through a deep conversation and generous affection. Put another way, men love through sex. Women desire emotional closeness, as do men, but for men it is achieved through the sexual act. Women's experience of love should not be considered more important than the male's experience of love. Within holy matrimony, God wants you to grow together as a couple. He wants you to meet your husband's needs and he to meet yours.

Your Husband's Desire

Your husband desires sex. Do not be misled; he desires the meaningful connection he experiences through sex as well as every part of that physical experience with you. His desire is not dirty or negative. Just as you may desire connection through generous affection and conversation. God designed both male and female with these desires because both are vital to a healthy, committed, and intimate marriage. Your husband desires you to fully love his body. He desires you to enjoy being with his body. He also really desires you to enjoy his intimate parts.

More than likely, your husband desires peni and wants you to enjoy giving it. For most men, this is a dream. If their wife does engage in this, it is a vital part of his lovemaking. I'll share with you some steamy insight into my own love life, here. I quizzed my husband to find out exactly how important oral is to him. Now, my husband is normally a pretty relaxed guy. But I was surprised at his enthusiasm in telling me. He said it is one of the most important things we do. His primary love language is acts of service. I'm not sure he would admit this, but as a wife, there are some things you just notice. The dishes get done, the trash goes out, he cleans the house without prompting practically proportionate to how often I serve him in this way. We can let this be our little secret, dear reader.

Notes from Ms. Susan:

How important do you think passion is in a marriage?

I think it's HUGE. We have a very physical relationship. We still watch movies arm in arm or his arm is around me and I'm curled into him. And we still hold hands. We still sleep very closely together. Even when it's really hot. Even when we're sick. We've never slept apart. Ever, I don't think. Not while at home at least.

I think that physical bond is a critical piece in staying intimate in your marriage. I would say that that is especially true. If one of you or your partner's love languages is physical touch. And it might not be. For both of us, it's quality time. And we have others that are secondary that are different for each of us. That is probably part of the reason our marriage has done as well as it has. I have made an effort to spend quality time with my husband.

Steamy JoDo:

Make an effort to touch your husband more; i.e., grab his hand when walking together, give him a short back rub when sitting near him, and lean against his chest when watching a show together.

Our Background Affects
Our Views of Sex

Issues From Childhood

As women, it's easy to think that sex is nasty or dirty. Many of us grew up with that notion. It's not really our parents' faults. They were probably just trying to protect us. They wanted to keep us from exploring too much. Your mom may have been clueless how to describe sex to you and thought the best thing to do for now is just it's "bad". You may have been told that it was nasty; that you shouldn't touch that area; that the girls that move their body like that or wear those clothes are sinful. Your parents were informed by their parents, their culture, and many other reasons. The way they talked about sex to you (or didn't) had a great effect. Even your parents' sexual relationship between each other have had untold effects on you, whether you know it or not. Their view of sex colors your own understanding of how sex "should" be.

As a kid, your parents teach you your colors, right from wrong, and what sex is. We took all those as unquestionable truths at the time. Now as adults we must go back, sort through, and rewrite our understandings where there is falsehood. In our late teens and early 20s many of us began to break from the systems of thought our parents laid out for us then. In college, I remember being shocked at how I had been raised to understand certain topics. As my understanding and awareness expanded, I had to realize some of what I had believed since childhood was not an appropriate belief at all. I began to question things I thought were right for so long. I even argued with others as a kid about these beliefs, and in college I realized I was wrong. It was painful to peel back the layers that were clouding my vision. As adults, this peeling back and correcting our opinions and thoughts should be an ongoing process. If we do not consciously question and rewrite our views, the automatic associations we were given from our family of origin will continue to affect us. Our job is to forge our own thinking and decide what *we* believe. That is part of God's plan as are "transformed by the renewing of your mind. Then you will be able to test and approve what God's will is--his good, pleasing and perfect will." (Romans 12:2).

A sad truth is that many of you, dear readers, were the victims of sexual abuse. The holy experience of sex that should be the utmost pleasure for you speaks of untold misery and heartache. I am so sorry that this has happened to you. God is angry that it did. You did not deserve it. A child or adult is never to be blamed at this kind of treatment. Though I have not walked in your shoes, I am praying that God would heal every atom of your heart and bring you to wholeness. God says that vengeance is the Lord's and He promises that He will judge accordingly. The hurt and pain that you carry is deep. You should take time to delve into its effects and what ways it affects your current view of sex. I would encourage seeking out a Christian counselor to help you through this process. Continually, give this issue to God. Continue to talk to Him about your hurt and struggle. He wants to heal and restore you to wholeness. God can use a mature friend whom you can be fully honest with and share your story to provide healing as well. Have you shared any abuse in your past with your husband? He should also know. Him loving you through this pain may be a vital piece in healing from it. Please, do not let someone's sin rob you of the true pleasure and joy purposed through marital intimacy. There is healing for you.

Perhaps before we even heard the story of Adam and Eve, we understood taking off our clothes was sinful. Write in your Workbook #3. Can you identify when you saw or heard that sex was bad? Was it just never talked about, except maybe in an R-rated movie? What subconscious messages did this send to you as a girl about sex?

We're Not Fine

Our parents were probably just trying to protect us and keep us from messing around before the appropriate time. Maybe their parents told them just as little and "they turned out fine". Well, when our nation's marriages are in crisis, far too many mothers are raising kids by themselves, men are avoiding popping the question like the plague… "turning out fine" is not good enough. This is *not* "fine". A friend of mine confided that her boyfriend is petrified that after they get married, they'll soon after stop having sex. My friend and her boyfriend have never slept together. He is just assuming it will happen because he's heard this so many times from his married friends. This fear is not uncommon. If we're "fine" in how we think about sex, talk about sex and teach our children about sex, then the status quo should also be "fine", but it is far from it. We need to start talking about sex (and the reasons we are so uncomfortable talking about it) with our friends, our kids, and especially our spouses.

Parents

Something I had to grapple with is my mother's view of sex. I don't really know about my parents sex life. Like you, it's something I try to avoid thinking about, actually. I did pick up some clues along the way.

Clue 1-My mom was never comfortable talking about it. I don't blame her for being uncomfortable. No mother wants to consider her beloved child having sex. So, on my own, I found out about sex, condoms, and how babies were made. After a boy made fun of me in class for not knowing what a "boner" was in 7th grade, I got mad at my mom. How could she let me experience such humiliation just because she didn't want to go through the mild embarrassment of explaining? I asked a girlfriend who gave me the low-down. It wasn't that I just didn't know the term, I didn't know that penises were anything more than pee dispensers.

Clue 2-My mom became visibly uncomfortable any time the subject came up. It seemed that she clearly disapproved of the conversation or question. I remember once she found a list a friend and I wrote of questions we had about boys and their anatomy. She probably didn't want my curiosity to turn into actions and I was punished. I felt like my curiosity was a sin. She was the one teaching me about God, how to be a friend of Jesus, and she taught me that all things related to sex were bad and sinful.

Clue 3-Though my parents had children, I sometimes wonder when. I can remember only once when their bedroom door was locked. Most of the time, if I (or any of us) had a nightmare, couldn't sleep, or wanted to tell mom something, we'd have free access to waltz into their bedroom to wake her. That was very kind of her to be available to her kids but I wonder if it made marital intimacy extra challenging.

Write your Workbook #4. Take a moment and fill out the following
    1) How did you think about sex growing up?
    2) What was your primary care taker's opinion of sex?
    3) Though I'm sure you would rather not think about it, what do you know of your parent's sexual relationship---healthy or not?

4) When you first heard of peni, what did you think? What do you think now of this sexual experience?

5) Are there other experiences that play into your current opinion?

Writing Or Trying To Write Over

I'll share my earliest sexual experience that shaped a lot of my views about sex. In high school, I was in a Civics class and we were each given a person to research. I was given Muhammad Ali. I was researching on the internet about "famous men" and other similar keywords for my paper. I distinctly remember clicking on a seemingly benign link about men. Many naked and sexual images came up. I was shocked. I had never experienced anything like this. Seeing the images made my body feel so unusual. I never knew that something visual could provide a physical response. I was so curious. After the shock passed, I came to a (sad) epiphany: here was a way to learn about sex without humiliating myself when I turned up at school ignorant. I knew it was wrong, but I remember feeling justified that I could attain sexual understanding through the worldwide web. Each picture was explaining something about which I was completely oblivious. Unfortunately, it instead provided many false ideas and sinful views of a perverted version of marital intimacy. I wish I could say that weeknight stumbling upon that site was the last time I looked at porn. I wish the ensuing years did not turn into a battle of my conscience and my sexual curiosity. I prayed many times and asked God for help. Years into this addiction, thank God, He did deliver me. It was a process. Pivotal steps were sharing with other Christians this struggle and asking for prayer and accountability. By God's grace, for years now I can confidently surf the internet without the slightest memory or desire to look into this again. But, only by God's powerful intervention and deliverance, can I--as can anyone with this struggle--do this.

I tell this experience with a heavy heart because we just have no idea how many children have similar stories. Sadly "90% of children between ages of eight and sixteen have viewed pornography on the Internet, in most cases unintentionally" [5]. Furthermore, their curiosity gets stoked and the internet provides quick and graphic answers. Maybe my mom was supposed to have clued me in, but instead Google was my teacher. As a side note, we as parents need to be vigilant for our children's purity. Put internet blocks on your children's TVs, phones, and computers. It is worth the money and minor struggle in order to protect their purity.

Please, *talk* to your kids about sex. It's so much easier to write on a blank slate than try to write over what the world has already written there. Friends of mine started talking to their kids as early as 4 years old. Now both daughters are entering college with full understanding of what many men want when they invite them to a party or their apartment. Knowledge like that is powerful. Those girls have the opportunity to make the decision to say "no" years in advance. Instead of figuring out in the moment, that boy didn't really want to show them "his DVD collection" and then having to decide if she should or shouldn't do what he wants. Give your kids the tools to remain pure. Tools of knowledge and understanding. If they understood, "Sex is all around us. This is what it means. Marriage is the best context. There is a lot of emptiness and heartbreak outside of marriage. But it is an incredible experience in marriage and you have the opportunity to wait". That can save them so much more than we know.

Notes From Ms. Susan:

I started off on the wrong track very much the same way you did. Early on, I read way too much of the wrong stuff, and thank God I didn't have the internet back then. So I didn't have to deal with that because it didn't exist. And so I learned the 'tricks of the trade' that way. But, I don't think our society gives us many other options. Which I think is really tragic.

Sin Discolors our Lense of God's Purity

I told you that my family of origin was a large factor in why I felt sex was wrong. But after being addicted to pornography, I despised my sin and judged every sexual act as a perversion. They reminded me of the perversion that I had seen. What I had witnessed *was* sin. But, after being delivered from the addiction, my mind and heart colored righteous, marital, sexual activity as sinful as well. I focused on running from sexual sin (as Paul encourages). But, when I was a young bride, I still associated holy intimacy in marriage as sin. This was a battle in my mind. I knew I wanted to please my husband, but I couldn't get my mind to shake this concern. I wanted to please God, so I was unable to fully engage in foreplay, the act, or any other part of the experience.

Write in your Workbook #5. Has your past sin colored your current view of sex?

Sexual perversions mimic what God intended to exist in a wonderful interaction within a specific environment. The problem is porn and other perversions destroy people's ability for intimacy. People who come out of the adult film industry have great difficulty having a healthy, monogamous life with someone. The number of adults addicted to porn is mind boggling. Sexual sin has infected and sickened our society. The sin of our society discolors what is God's purity in marriage. Many of us have--in reaction--come to associate what is good in marriage with sin. We have seen it practiced in the wrong environment. Sex is not bad, but God specifically set up the universe to work best when we limit sex to have with our husband for life.

Steamy To Do:

Treat your husband to a full-body massage (Feel free to do an internet search "how to give a full-body massage" first). While you're touching him, connect deeply with his body. Feel how wonderful his body is beneath your fingers. Silently, thank God for his skin, muscles, bones, strength, and every other part of God's creation right here beneath your hands. Enjoy those very attractive areas you love so much.

Oral Sex, Sinful?

God's Laws

As Christians, we are to be in the world and not of it, we must rise above and often ignore the expectations of our society. However, Christianity is really not about rules. It is about a relationship with God. He is completely holy and perfect. Our sin separates us from God, but Jesus' sacrifice was to give us a relationship with God. As we walk with God, we come to learn what He cares about. In His wisdom, He made the world hang on particular laws--He set it up for friendship, relationship, and marriages to work according to certain guidelines. God gives some parameters but outside of those, He does not limit our exploration and pursuits to understand and enjoy His universe. We have to be careful not to think of the Bible as a rule book. It is a gracious gift by which we can know the Father and understand His ways and His world.

Many laws and truths are elucidated in His Word, but not all. Gravity is not found in the Bible, but that is part of His design of the world. He has specific truths in His Word, but He also gives us freedom to discover the vast universe He designed outside of those. That is why we look at scientific as well as experiential wisdom, anchored by biblical wisdom in this course.

The Bible Says

God in His infinite wisdom does have purposes for sex and there are ways he says it can be misused. God provides guidelines around sexual relationships. There are specific ways God instructs us to utilize this powerful tool of sex. I'd like to paraphrase parts of the authors of *Intimate Issues* [6] exploration of the Bible. They searched the scriptures and noted each place guidelines around sex were given.

Here are the areas that scripture prohibits.

1. Fornication: sex outside of marriage (1 Cor 7:2; 5:1; 6:13-16; 1Thess 4:3; Matt 5:32)

2. Adultery: sex with anyone who is not your spouse, in deed or heart (Lev 20:10; Matt 5:28)

3. Homosexuality: sex with persons of same genitalia (Lev 18:22; 20:13; Rom 1:27; 1 Cor 6:9)

4. Impurity: lose virginity due to living pagan lifestyle (1 Cor 6:9; 2 Cor 7:1; Rev 14:4; 22:11)

5. Orgies or Swinging: violates #1, 2 & 4.

6. Prostitution: paying for sex (Lev 19:29; Deut 23:17; Prov 7:4-27)

7. Lustful Passions & Sexual Fantasies: unrestrained sexual passion for anyone other than the person's marriage partner; sexual fantasies outside of your marital union (Matt 5:28; Mark 7:21-22; Eph 4:19)

8. Sodomy aka unnatural sexual intercourse, ie: sex with someone of same genitalia, temple prostitutes or animals (Deut 23:17, Kings 14:24)

9. Incest: sex with family members or relatives (Lev 18:7-18; 20:11-21)

10. Pornography: violates #2, 4, 6 & 7

Now that we have looked at exactly what God's boundaries are for marriage, where God draws the line, we need to clarify what *is* OK. Well, basically, everything else. Within your marriage, physical intimacy can be enjoyed by you and your husband. In every area of life, within God's parameters, He gives us a lot of freedom. He wants us to enjoy the breadth and width of His creation. Within the bounds of marriage, we can enjoy the fruits of His creation (ie your husband) in *every way*. Let's use another example. I have never seen ice cream mentioned in the Bible. But God created everything we need to produce ice cream and I credit God for intending it for my enjoyment. It probably would have been mentioned had there been freezers back then. I imagine Jesus and I would have shared this sweet passion.

I have never questioned whether God approved of my enjoying this pleasure. Now, if I over-indulge that would cross God's boundary: do not be given to gluttony (Prov 23:2). That is His parameter, but within that guidance, I could eat ice cream in a cone, with chocolate sauce, with a side of bacon, or any other way my heart desired. He knows what is best and He gives parameters accordingly. He knows that if I ate ice cream all day, and lived gluttonously in regards to this pleasure, I would be miserable and would not fulfill His purposes for me on this earth. However, within that guideline, I can deeply enjoy his gift of ice cream. Use the guidelines above to consider what is sin and what is *not* in your sexual activities.

I'm Not Sure I'm Comfortable

It is ok if you're not comfortable. It is ok that you feel uncomfortable with particular bedroom activities, namely peni. I think it is a mistake for us to only say "if you feel comfortable with peni, go for it". None of us feel comfortable with things we do not understand or have never done before. So many women would like to feel comfortable, if someone just told them what the heck to do down there! Just because something is uncomfortable for you now, does not mean it should be. You picked up this book because you desire to get to a place where you do feel comfortable. Maybe your husband has brought it up to you and you've declined because of your comfort level or your concern with its righteousness. We'll be going into other fears associated with this experience soon. Do not think that your level of comfort should dictate what you can or cannot do in the bedroom. New activities are always uncomfortable, mentally and emotionally. You will have to fight through the discomfort to get to the *immense* pleasure of peni. There is so much pleasure and purpose awaiting your marriage if you begin taking those (temporarily) uncomfortable steps.

Biblical Oral Sex

Have you ever read the Song Of Solomon in the Bible? Maybe it would surprise you to know that it is an erotic exchange between two lovers. It contains beautiful imagery and poetry that speak of many ways two lovers enjoy each other sexually. It even specifically alludes to peni. "Like an apple tree among the trees of the woods, So is my beloved among the sons. I sat down in his shade with great delight, And his fruit was sweet to my taste" (Song of Solomon 2:3). Many scholars believe this is speaking of peni. Bible Commentator Joseph Dillow compares the text with extra biblical literature in which "fruit is sometimes equated with the male genitals or with semen, so it is possible that here we have a faint and delicate reference to an oral genital caress" [7]. Furthermore, in Song of Solomon 4:16, Solomon's wife says "Awake, O north *wind,* And come, O south! Blow upon my garden, That its spices may flow out. Let my beloved come to his garden and eat its pleasant fruits". Pastor, Mark Driscoll says "the husband likens his wife's unclothed body to a garden filled with delightful scents and flavors... the wife invites him to perform peni" [8].

Isn't the biblical imagery in Song of Solomon beautiful? This is a holy and wonderful exchange between husband and wife. Also, did you notice the female voice is taking the lead in these seductions? Be encouraged that God gives you the green light to be just as seductive and forward with your hubby.

(Even more so.) I'm not sure how this book was written but she probably knew others would be reading it and had to be more tight-lipped than she would be in her lover's embrace.

Your husband would really enjoy the opportunity to relax and let his incredible wife lead. Men by social conditioning often feel a strong pressure to perform during sex. If you are having trouble with your husband initiating, or in the way he chooses to, it may be that he feels the pressure to be perfect or in-charge. Alleviate this by taking the lead yourself, like Solomon's wife. Allow him to relax and take the reins yourself. The Song of Solomon's wife wasn't shy and I'm sure Solomon was very appreciative.

Oral Sex Is Part of a Godly Experience

The Bible was written in a very different time and culture than what we see around us. Since we are living in our current time and using this frame of reference to understand God and His values, we have an added challenge to understand its meanings. In this day and age, we are using society's frame of reference to judge something God created. I will clarify. In Bible times, people didn't categorize sex in specific ways as we do now, ie: foreplay, oral, intercourse, anal etc. You won't find these distinctions in the Bible. We use them in our terminology as a clarification of the lovemaking experience. But these should not be considered separate. In Solomon's day they didn't ask "if peni was a sin"--because as you can see in the above verses, peni was part of the beautiful and holy act within a marital union. When two people become one flesh, *every part* of one is now part of the other. *Every part* are united. *Every part* should be enjoyed in the passion of love making. When you are loving on your husband intimately, that is just another expression of union and love. If you had the question: "is *peni* with my husband a sin?" Because peni was just a part of sex in Bible times, that question wouldn't make sense. The only question that would make sense would have been: "is *sex* with my husband a sin?" Let's dive into this question now. To get at the heart of this concern, we have to recognize the real way we *see* sex.

God Doesn't See Sex Like Our Society Does

Something has gotten twisted. Something has gone terribly wrong in our understanding of sex. Maybe it started because of the fall of Adam & Eve. That's why we are embarrassed to talk to our kids about it. That's why we think certain acts are dirty and sinful. That's why so many marriages lack a zestful, fun, and exhilarating sexual intimacy. As Christian women, in light of God's glory, we have become *ashamed* of sex. This is not God's will. Let's look at Genesis 2:24 in the Amplified Version "Therefore a man shall leave his father and his mother and shall become united and cleave to his wife, and they shall become one flesh. And the man and his wife were both naked and were not embarrassed or ashamed in each other's presence." It is interesting to me that the verse specifies after becoming "one flesh" they were "both naked and were not embarrassed or ashamed".

Back In The Garden

Imagine for a moment you are Eve. You are the only woman on earth. In fact, aside from animals and trees, there is no one except your husband. Imagine your husband is Adam. You and your husband physically become "one flesh" frequently. You might have various favorite gardens in which you tease and frolic with each other. On a particularly gorgeous afternoon, you're sitting and relaxing on the bank of a beautiful stream. You're leaning against a great oak with your toes in the cool water, enjoying the warm sun on your face. Your husband startles you by quietly approaching and kissing you on the neck. He presents the most beautiful bouquet. "These reminded me of you, baby. Love you." These breathtaking flowers, you know he spent the better part of the day carefully searching out, considering your favorites, and only choosing the most perfect blossoms. You wrap your arms around him and he kisses you deeply on the lips. After a moment, you slip under his arm and skip away, glancing over your shoulder with a 'come and get me' smile. He knows this game and he starts after as you pick up the pace. You can feel your heart beating fast as you move your feet over the cushy forest floor as quickly as they'll go. Though you know all the best routes, after a couple of moments, he inevitably catches up, grabs your waist, and playfully tackles you. You fall down on the soft grass with such glee and you both laugh heartily and enjoy his embrace. He begins to kiss your neck and moves to your chest then continues down. He is caring, tender and gentle. You feel free and loved and passionate in this experience. Fully imagine yourself in this scene.

Basking in the afterglow of intimate passion, you're resting together, lying on his chest. Imagine you both glance up and see God walking towards you. You eagerly welcome Him to sit beside you. What a wonderful surprise to have God visit. You genuinely exclaim, "So glad you stopped by! We just had a glorious afternoon, God. I am in complete awe of how you've made my husband. He's so incredible. Every part of him and his heart brings me such joy. Did you see the flowers he gave me?" You show Him the marvelous bouquet. "Well, I really should be thanking You for all of these delights, shouldn't I?" All of you laugh. God looks at you with such deep tenderness and love. He is happy with you. He delights in you. You are happy with Him. You are grateful for what He has given you. He has given you these incredible gifts. He has given you your husband. He has made every part of your husband. And it brings God delight that you enjoy His creation. He loves to hear your appreciation in act and word of His handiwork. It brings Him joy to see you cherish what he has made in your husband.

Write in your Workbook #6. Were you able to see yourself as Eve? What emotions came up when you considered God walking in? What does this clue you in to your own views of God's purpose for sex?

God Is Present

If you could visualize yourself in this story, I'm interested if it startled you when I mentioned God walking in on you? I must ask: why? God made it all. He sees it all. He made you to sexually crave your husband. This is *His* design. His idea. He made your intimate places. He knows you completely. He designed your vagina to become moist, sensitive, and elongated in preparation for your husband's erect penis. These things don't surprise Him. He is responsible for the tickle you feel when your clitoris becomes enlarged awaiting your husband's gentle touch. Do you think He doesn't know or doesn't care? When we see God as our designer and creator, we are more able to understand how Adam and Eve were naked and unashamed. They were not ashamed of their sexuality. It was another wonderful gift that God had given them. Just as the flowers, fruit trees, and deer were all gifts, so too was their intimate experience.

Maybe you want to protest. "Eve was sinless, of course she could have sex in front of God and not be ashamed. There's too much sin in me and my past to be able to understand sex as pure and holy". Before the fall she was sinless, yes. But, none of us deserve to commune with God based on our own perfection. None of us. The Bible says "all our righteous acts are like filthy rags" (Isaiah 64:6). On our own we are completely filthy, totally unworthy of God's attention. Only because of Jesus are we given freedom from our sin. If we accept Jesus' sacrifice, God does not even remember our sin (Hebrews 8:12). Daily we are to renew our minds, purify our hearts, and become more like Him. I believe part of that purification is putting sex in its proper place in our mind. Just as every deed and action should come from a heart wanting to honor God, sex should also be engaged with that heart. Let me be clear. You are not sinning by making love to your husband. You are not sinning by all types of passionate, fun, generous expressions of love with your husband.

Give God Glory For Sex

Sex is part of God's plan and design for you both. If we feel guilty in our times of sexual intimacy, we are robbing God of the glory He is due in this area. When you have an appropriate understanding of God's purposes of sex, it can free you up to love God more because of the experience.

When I visited the Grand Canyon my heart was moved with the glory and power of God. I felt more in love with Him when I recognized His awesome creation and gave Him glory for it. In the same way, every time you orgasm and feel an indescribable release and pleasure, you should be grateful to God. God made that. He deserves your thanks for it. When you see sex as God's gift to you, engaging in pleasurable love making is also drawing you closer to God in gratitude and worship. Sex is an important part of your life and you should recognize God is part of this experience. He should be glorified in your bedroom.

Write in your Workbook #7. What areas of your sexuality have you not acknowledged as God's plan? Give God praise for His amazing design of sex for you. Pray with me: *God, help me to see sex as a gift from you to be enjoyed and indulged in with my husband. Help me to see our intimacy as truly your design for my life and marriage. Amen.*

God Made Your Husband's Parts

Funnily enough, God gave you hunger and thirst. It is funny we do not spend time focusing on *if* we should enjoy the pleasures that come with taste, smell, or feelings of fullness. When our appetites are filled, we thank God for supplying them. We even pray at every meal in gratitude and seeking His blessing as we consume His creation. Think of how much of our lives revolve around these enjoyments: coffee dates, candle lit dinners, cold cut lunches, and indulgent desserts. Within the context of gratefulness to God for these delights (staying within the previously mentioned boundaries) we are totally at peace enjoying His provision.

We have the wrong view of sex if we do not think it appropriate to do the same with another God-given kind of appetite. He made your husband's very sensitive penis and testes. They are wonderful opportunities for you to love your husband, given by God. God intended Adam to desire an intimate connection with Eve. God knows and loves your husband completely. He made your husband to crave your sexual touch. God is responsible for your husband's sexual appetite and desires. In fact, God made it so when you walk in the room in a revealing outfit, your husband's mind becomes excited and his member begins to grow in length and stiffness. God created Adam and Eve to become one flesh, be naked, and be unashamed. It is only sin that makes this understanding of God's will hard to accept. Yes, there is sin that we've experienced in one way or another distorting our understanding of our husband's sexual cravings. As you become acquainted with this in your mind, I wonder if there is something fighting you from receiving this as true?

Write in your Workbook #8. Would you write in your workbook any reservations you have in believing God designed your husband's genitals to work in the way they do? As you get clear on the reservations you have, I also want you to pray about it. Ask God to reveal His truth to you. Ask Him to erase the sin-tainted views of oral and all other sexual acts.

What God Really Thinks

God uses the sexual relationship between husband and wife to analogize His depth of love and desire for intimacy with us. It may be shocking, but it is true. Check out the book of Hosea. God specifically tells the prophet, Hosea, to go marry a prostitute, so that Hosea might understand how deeply God is hurt by Israel's unfaithfulness to Him. The Bible talks about believers as Jesus' bride who He is perfecting to be without spot or blemish on the wedding day (aka a virgin) (2 Cor 11:2, Eph 5:32). The Holy Spirit came upon Mary and impregnated her so that Jesus would be born (Matt :18). Furthermore, circumcision was God's symbolic sign of Israel's love and commitment to Him. It was at the very point of a man's sexuality--his penis--that had to be cut to confirm their devotion to God (Deut 10:16, Eph 5:32).

God understands fiery passion. He understands the jealousy that goes with the sexual relationship. He feels deeply in love with us in this way. He repeatedly involves the analogy of sex to let us see just how deeply, passionately, and completely He cares for us. He is talking about something holy, wonderful, and righteous: sex. He is talking about His design. "'For this reason a man shall leave his father and mother and be joined to his wife, and the two shall become one flesh.' This is a great mystery, but I speak concerning Christ and the church." (Eph 5:31-32). Pastor Tim Keller, says "Sex is for fully committed relationships because it is a foretaste of the joy that comes from being in complete union with God through Christ. The most rapturous love between a man and a woman on earth is only a hint of what that is like" [9].

The deeper we go with God in this area, the more He will reveal this holy act of love and commitment. As you and I are open to God redeeming our minds and hearts to His sexual design, I believe there will be more revelation in our hearts. In The Gift of Sex, Penner says "Most of the time we let our minds control us. But in the moment of orgasm, we are released from that control; climax is something that we experience as a totality. Everything about us enters into it. Perhaps this is how the sexual experience represents our relationship to God. In this total, intense fusion of body, emotion, and spirit, we are connected with what it can be like to be totally one with God. This is indeed a mystery" [10]. The most relevant point to recognize is sex in all its forms--within His boundaries--is God-designed and ordained.

Steamy To Dos:

Take the lead one time this week. Confidently initiate lovemaking. Begin a makeout session where you begin to pull off his shirt and continue to move things further. Give your husband the gift of taking the lead, like the wife in the Song of Solomon.

God's Purposes For Sex

God's Truth

God made Adam and had complete access to him. They walked together in the cool of the day. I can only imagine the friendship they shared. I look forward to heaven to experience such incredible friendship with God. But, as God looked upon Adam, He said it is "not good for man to be alone" (Gen 2:18). God made Eve, because he didn't want Adam to be alone. As the master creator of everything and every part of our bodies, he told them to "be fruitful and multiply" (Gen 1:28). God provided only one way to do this: sex. Here we can see both pieces of God's plan playing out in our lives. The relational piece, often more represented in of females' needs, is captured in God's mention "it is not good for man to be alone". Adam needs companionship and love. He needs someone to support him, to stretch him, to compliment his strengths, and to walk alongside him through life. The sexual piece often more represented in the needs of males is captured in God's command to "be fruitful and multiply". Have sex and have babies.

God made the process of making children incredibly pleasurable. Interestingly, it wasn't until the fall that the curse made it challenging to actually birth children. Many well-meaning Christians throughout church history believed that sex is only for procreation. They believe that God intended people to have sex, if and only if, they are trying to have a baby. But, if that's true, why isn't sex under this curse of pain, like child birthing is? If sex equates to having children, it should be under the same curse as birthing the child is. Furthermore, when a couple is "trying to get pregnant" they usually try for months, at least. If God wanted us to have sex only to have a baby and wanted us to avoid it otherwise, why wouldn't he make a more exact process? God could have made the process simple, foolproof, and not require a frequent sexual experience. Other processes in the body work much more effectively. For example, if we have not consumed enough Vitamin C, all we have to do is consume an orange and voila! Our body receives, processes, and utilizes the introduced vitamin immediately. This is not the case for eggs and sperm. There are dozens, maybe hundreds, of factors that are necessary for conceiving a child. Conceiving a child is a mysterious and incredible part of a process of intimate experience with your husband. After conception, there is a long, 9-month period of needing support and service, providing a continuation of the knowledge and growing-together process.

God included sex in many areas of the Bible as a natural, normal, and regular part of a marital relationship. God made certain visuals, certain caresses, and certain stimulations very pleasurable. We, sinful humans, didn't make this thing up. *God* created sex. I imagine that my loving Heavenly Father would have smiled when I innocently asked my mother about my sexual curiosities. He also made this topic incredibly interesting to us, even as children. It is a wonderful thing that should be anticipated, patiently waited for, and always held in high-regard. It is truly a gift. When I was a child asking my innocent questions, I think God would have scooped me up, sat me on his lap, and warmly explained His incredible design for our bodies and sexual pleasure. It is *right*. It is *His* beautiful and holy design. At that age, I would have needed to wait but in anticipation for an incredible experience awaiting my marital union.

Sex Unifies

Sadly, our society thinks the purpose of sex is personal pleasure. As such, we have unattached people sleeping together calling it 'friends with benefits.' A night of partying ends in 'hooking up' with some stranger, because it *feels good*. But that is not the reason God created sex. At the heart of God is unification in marriage. A process of becoming one. Even in the beginning of Genesis, God says man and wife should become "one flesh". The act of sex as a becoming one flesh rings true in my experience. When my husband and I are frequently making love generously, we are connected on a level that is unlike any other time and unlike a connection with anyone else. Even lying there in the afterglow of sex, there's a freedom and unity between us that is practically tangible. Pleasure is a wonderful aspect and should be fully enjoyed. But the pleasure is part of the unifying experience that is sex. God's intention for sex is solidifying and strengthening the husband and wife's "oneness".

If our culture could understand sex as unifying two people this significantly, I don't think they would handle sex so loosely. Since our society says pleasure is the purpose of sex, it cheapens the depth of the experience. Look what Paul says on this, "Do you not know that he who unites himself with a prostitute is one with her in body? For it is said, 'The two will become one flesh'" (1Cor 6:16). When people have sex outside of marriage, it damages the heart. People *do* become unified through this act, but do not respect it as such. Our society tries to interpret this experience as just for individual enjoyment, but it is not so simple. A person who continues having casual sex numbs and calluses a vital part of his or her heart. Unifying themselves to many different people and not sustaining unity with any causes great destruction. With a deep understanding of God's true design and purpose of sex, and knowing the difference this understanding makes, I grieve for others who consider sex so lightly. Whatever your past, God can heal, renew, and restore. I believe He will do that with your marriage. You have the opportunity to share in a journey with your husband in unity and pleasure with your beloved in God's adventures.

Write in your Workbook #9. When you consider the sex act as a means for unifying you and your husband, does it shift the way you may esteem this part of your life?

Marriage Lets Us Love Others More

I am going to share with you a part of my past for which I needed forgiveness. I want to be transparent and vulnerable with you, so that you feel empowered to also be honest with yourself. How can I expect you to look at the harsh realities of your situation if I act like I have lived a perfect life and have no need of God's grace? If you can relate, I want you to know that you're not alone and God can redeem. God has brought me out of many pits of sin. God taught me that sex within the proper bounds of marriage provides the appropriate place for my sexual desires to be filled. This is a wonderful thing. As we enjoy this marvelous part of life, our focus is freed up to be on others and His work in the Kingdom much more.

When D and I met, I had moved far from the Lord. I was not going to church, praying, or allowing the truth in God's word have authority in my thoughts or any part of life. Sex was one of the largest sources of pain--not pleasure--in my failed marriage. I had been hurt by Christians and felt like they were wrong in how they viewed sex. I was very hurt and was not looking for anything other than a fling, an adrenaline rush, and something to boost my needy ego. So, D and I slept together very soon into our relationship. He was an amazing man and fell in love with him soon into dating. As I grew in my love and emotional stability, God started drawing me and D to Himself.

We started going to a church in our city, but I really couldn't engage as I felt guilt over our sexual relationship. After moving because of my job and two years into our relationship, we got married. Then, we started going to a church in our new area. God showed up for both of us so powerfully. I felt a connectedness to Him and a desire to live for something more than myself. I was baptized in that church (after my childhood baptism) and I decided to recommit my life to Christ wholly and completely. My husband made the same decision 10 months later. God was so kind to bring us both to Himself. I know many of you are praying for your husband's salvation. I want to encourage you to keep praying and keep loving *hard.* Our God is faithful. As my pastor encouraged me before D had gotten to this step: "you want your husband to see that you becoming a Christian is the *best* thing to ever happen to your marriage". What a vision for women who are believing for change in their marriage!

In looking at the trajectory of our relationship, D and I were reflecting on how God has changed us and redeemed our relationship. It is pretty incredible to realize that God has brought both of us out of addictions, destructive coping habits, self-loathing, very painful pasts, destructive communication, and many selfish pursuits. In thinking about the good we were doing in others' lives during our dating period, I must say there isn't much. We were so self-serving. We were so selfish. Our thoughts were constantly about ourselves and trying to make ourselves happy. We'd have a lot of fights that were rooted in self-serving desires. There were a lot of fun moments, but there wasn't a lot purpose or caring for anyone outside of each other.

Now, God has given us the grace to do life with others, to serve and love people in an active way and according to each of our strengths. D is an amazing servant, he thrives at loving others through acts of service. Being in a growing and thriving church community, D is able to help people move, setup for Sunday services, and he is often assisting others who need a helping hand. I am able to serve in the ways God leads me through leading groups on prayer, Bible studies, and connecting with attendees one-on-one who need a listening ear. It's amazing how much good God allows us to be a part of. It is incredible how our relationship no longer inhibits this kind of action, but supports and encourages it.

Healthy Marriage Supports God's Plans

When our relationship was on really rough ground, it consumed my thoughts. I was constantly pursuing my own pleasure or happiness in our relationship, it was an empty pursuit. As God has changed and is continuing to change my mind about how I should be in this marriage, my life has drastically changed.

Paul says "But I say to the unmarried and to widows that it is good for them if they remain even as I. But if they do not have self-control, let them marry; for it is better to marry than to burn with passion." (1 Corinthians 7:8-9). To me, this verse means that our lives were perfectly whole as single people. You may have even been able to accomplish more in the Kingdom of God with all that time not devoted to another person's care. But, many of us could not sustain that kind of a life. Paul seems to say, "if you cannot flourish in singleness, then do not delay. Stop wasting energy trying to resist the benefits of marriage. Get married so you can get on with the business God has for you. Don't spend time being distracted by this idol of marriage. Select a worthy suitor, make the commitment, and get on with what God wants you to be doing."

As you dig deep in your marriage, realize the rewards are exponential. You are not digging deep just to have a happier marriage. By caring for your mate and investing time and effort into him, you will also have the ability to do more of God's work together. Your mind is freed up to be focused on what God wants you to do. Someone who is stressed about their spouse will spend far more time trying to get out of that stress through their coping mechanism of choice, ie: alcohol, eating, TV, reading, depressive thoughts, complaining, etc. All of that takes precious time, energy, and focus away from the purposes God has for you. It also makes for a toxic mind that will not be walking according to the Spirit. Take the time to invest into the health and vitality of your marriage, for God's sake.

Loving Your Husband as Devotion to God

God gives us a lot of freedom to enjoy His creation. He gives us a lot of joys around us. If you have kids, you can recognize the joy that God's incredible creation brings you. If you've ever witnessed a breathtaking sunset, you understand the awe God brings us when admiring His creation. If you've ever traveled to a natural wonder, like Yellowstone, the Redwood Forests, or Big Sur and felt consumed with the greatness of God, you understand the fullness of heart you feel when appreciating God's work. Enjoying and beholding His glory in each creation is an act of worship and connection to The Holy.

Appreciating and loving your husband is an act of worship. "Truly I tell you, anyone who gives you a cup of water in my name because you belong to the Messiah will certainly not lose their reward" (Mark 9:41). Loving and serving your husband is an act of worship. "Love your neighbor as yourself" (Matt 22:39). The posture of your heart toward your husband is an act of worship. When you "in humility value others above yourselves", you are participating in an act of worship (Phil 2:3). When loving your husband, you're also loving God.

Write in your Workbook #10. Consider the ways in which the unhealthy parts of your marriage are absorbing much of your energy. Dream of ways to renew those areas of your marriage. Dream about your life and about God's purposes that you can accomplish when your marriage is on more solid ground.

God's Love Multiplies

There's something truly remarkable in the way God set up the universe. He said it is not good for man to be alone and so He made Eve and married them. Yet, He also says we are to "Love the Lord your God with all your heart and with all your soul and with all your strength and with all your mind" (Luke 10:27). I find that remarkable because God made the world to work in perfect harmony. We can be in love with each other and simultaneously be completely in love with Him. A friend of mine with three grown children told me something quite profound. She shared, "It's funny. When I was pregnant with my second child, I remember worrying 'how can I possibly love this new child as much as I love my first?' But when my baby was born, somehow it made me love *both* of my children more". God designed the universe so love multiplies. God's love is endless and the more we love, the more it pours into us and out onto others. It's amazing that God set it up so our deep love for one child only increases as we love another. Similarly, our love for God increases our love for all else. Our love for our husbands can even increase our love for God. As I fall deeper in love with my husband on a daily basis, I can feel the love of God wash over me as I lean in and trust in this love. God wants to use our marriages to love Him and follow Him more.

Repentance to Become Free

If this seems impossible right now, there may be something hindering this experience. Become curious about your particular situation. It may be God is pointing out sin (in action or thought) that He is prompting you to a) change, b) repent of, and/or c) claim victory over. God loves you and desires to connect with us on *every* level. It is His kindness that leads us to repentance (Rom 2:4). Review the Bible passages included in the "The Bible Says" section above. Ask God to show you where you may need to change in your thought-life or actions. Surrender these sins to Him. Are their visuals, fantasies, or other areas that you have engaged in and need God's forgiveness? He is showing you these sins because He loves you. He wants to walk with you in a deeper way.

Write in your Workbook #11. Do you see areas of your sexuality that do not align with God's truth? Write about them.

Pray with me: *God, I worship you and thank you for loving me so completely. Lord, show me my sin that I may repent and walk more closely with you. Lord, forgive me of the sin of* [insert]. *Thank you for your gift of salvation and that your blood washes me whiter than snow. Lord help me to live in this truth, that you have forgiven me and do not even remember my faults. Thank you God for your freedom. I love you.*

Surrendering Our Views

Surrender any selfish view of sex. It may also be time to surrender the view that ignores God's plans and purposes for sex and assumes it is just for you (or just for your husband), instead of understanding it is an act *purposed* by God. Repent of the view that God doesn't belong in your marital intimacy.

Surrender the view that God is not interested or doesn't care about this area of your life. Surrender the view that He is mad at you in this area. The truth is God made this passion, pleasure, and energy for you and your husband to engage in together. If you have utilized it wrongly in the past, you are given the opportunity to give that wholly to God and ask for His forgiveness. He longs for you to humbly acknowledge His truth in this area and forgive you for these sins. He wants to make you completely clean in your heart. He made it all for a purpose. He wants you to enjoy this beautiful experience and invite Him into your thoughts and passion. This is something you need God's help to get right.

Write in your Workbook #12. In what ways do you need to surrender your thoughts, misunderstandings, or judgments of sex that are not aligned with God's heart and truth?

Pray with me: *Lord, I surrender my wrong thoughts about this amazing gift you have given me. Would you forgive me for* [insert]. *God would you correct my heart on this issue? Help me to love you and invite you into this area of my life that I have closed off from you for so long. Forgive me of influencing others incorrectly about this important topic. Thank you for your mercy. God change me into your image and help me to enjoy sex as you intended it. Help me to see your holy purposes for lovemaking.*

Eternal Rewards

"As iron sharpens iron, so one person sharpens another" (Prov 27:17). I find this scripture in the marital relationship. God wants us to sharpen each other and help each other to grow towards Him. Marriage brings out the worst and the best in us, pushes all our buttons, and tries our patience. It is all a journey of preparation, sacrifice, and love to be His bride (Eph 5:27). I don't understand what exactly will happen at the end of this life, but I do know God has big plans for us on the other side. What we spend time cultivating and developing in this life *will matter* in eternity.

I am no expert on eschatology, but the view that God has eternal assignments for us motivates me to live in pursuit of His holiness. In this life, we can either seek carnal desires or godly pursuits. "So we fix our eyes not on what is seen, but on what is unseen, since what is seen is temporary, but what is unseen is eternal." (2 Cor 4:18). As a wife, you are given the opportunity (probably multiple times every day) to develop your character, the fruits of the Spirit, and a Christ-like heart. Often this development comes through trials and challenges. Maybe an instance where you would normally respond with frustration and annoyance is an opportunity to strengthen your muscles of gentleness and kindness.

I want to bring this point about God developing your character into the bedroom. There are many times I am too tired, busy, sweaty, or just feeling too [fill-in-the-blank] to engage in sex. My husband respects that. But what about the times when I push through those reservations and decide I am going to invest in our marriage? My attitude is totally different by the end and I'm *glad* I did. Do you like to work out? Most of us groan, or, at least did at some point before it became a regular part of our lives. The way we get into the habit of working out takes concerted effort. We may have to drag ourselves to the gym, but a couple of minutes on that elliptical changes everything. By the time you've broken a sweat and started listening to your tunes, you're feeling vital and powerful. Pushing through the initial resistance is the key. The posture of my heart to move me from lethargy into action is something that is developing my character. When I choose to make love to my husband, I am developing my character, and actively investing in our marital unity and fruitful, Kingdom-centered marriage. I may have to initially commit to be a servant (without expectation or resentment). I am serving with a giving and loving heart. You may never know the benefits of investing in a sexual experience with your hubby, whether in this life or the next.

The Intention Of Love

You love your spouse. You may tell him every day as he leaves for work. Consider what actions are truly lining up with that. I strongly encourage you to have sex as an act of love and devotion to your husband and commitment to the health of your marriage. This is God's will for your lives together. I encourage you to do whatever is necessary to make sure that happens and regularly (we'll dive much deeper into this soon). Get yourself to a place where you initiate sex, where you give your husband great intimate pleasure, and where you feel free and whole to have a fantastic sex life.

Having said all of that, your intention--the posture of your heart--is *vital*. There are women who do a lot of kind things for their husbands, but they feel resentment in their hearts. Or they keep score. Or it is an act and they expect it will return to them somehow. I have been guilty of this myself. That is not the kind of action the Bible encourages. It is vital that your intention is love, *while* you're doing. Let's take a moment to dive into how scripture explains this. You're probably familiar with the famous "love chapter," 1 Corinthians 13:1-13. Read it again below, but pretend this is your first time hearing these words. Ask God to show you new things. Read slowly and consider afresh what it means for your marriage.

1"If I speak in the tongues of men or of angels, but do not have love, I am only a resounding gong or a clanging cymbal.

2 If I have the gift of prophecy and can fathom all mysteries and all knowledge, and if I have a faith that can move mountains, but do not have love, I am nothing.

3 If I give all I possess to the poor and give over my body to hardship that I may boast, but do not have love, I gain nothing.

4 Love is patient, love is kind. It does not envy, it does not boast, it is not proud.

5 It does not dishonor others, it is not self-seeking, it is not easily angered, it keeps no record of wrongs.

6 Love does not delight in evil but rejoices with the truth.

7 It always protects, always trusts, always hopes, always perseveres.

8 Love never fails. But where there are prophecies, they will cease; where there are tongues, they will be stilled; where there is knowledge, it will pass away.

9 For we know in part and we prophesy in part,

10 But when completeness comes, what is in part disappears.

11 When I was a child, I talked like a child, I thought like a child, I reasoned like a child. When I became a man, I put the ways of childhood behind me.

12 For now we see only a reflection as in a mirror; then we shall see face to face. Now I know in part; then I shall know fully, even as I am fully known.

13 And now these three remain: faith, hope and love. But the greatest of these is love"

Write in your Workbook #13. Jot down any new insights you gained from that reading. Did God show you anything about your marriage, and how you are to love for your husband?

I find it fascinating how Paul contrasts lots of actions with "love". Love is a word we usually think of as a feeling. Paul talks about action: we could *speak* in the tongues of angels, *search* out all knowledge and mysteries, *move* mountains with our faith, or *give* away everything to the poor. Then he says it is all nothing if we do not "have love". We can do a lot of good things in this world, even godly things. But by the end of our lives, could it all be considered "nothing"? This scripture makes it clear that love is a choice for *us* to make. It is our decision to put love into everything we are doing. It is vital. Paul gives us a warning. He doesn't want us to be ignorant. When we were children we thought like children--we didn't know any better. But as adults, we now know better. We have to take responsibility and choose to act in love.

This chapter makes it clear that love is something we need to a) understand and b) consciously infuse into our actions. As children we could get away with acting resentful. Children can without kindness, patience, truth, hope, and perseverance. Paul is telling us, "it is time to grow up. In the end it will matter."

Everything else in this book should be viewed as an outpouring of love for your husband. When I ask you to do *anything*, please remember to do it in love. Because it matters. Choose to get your heart right. Infuse love into all you do in your marriage, and strip off any attitude that is *not* love. Take this to heart. Love doesn't boast, envy, dishonor others, delight in evil. Love isn't self-seeking, prideful, easily angered and it keeps no record of wrongs. Love is kind, patient, it rejoices in the truth, always protects, trusts, hopes and perseveres; love never fails.

I'd like to also include the Delight Your Husband Version of this passage. "If I fold the laundry, keep the house immaculate, scrub the floors every night for 30 years of marriage, but have not love I am nothing. If I make an organic, balanced breakfast every morning and a five-star dining experience every night, but have not love I am nothing. If I am always the "go to" woman in my church or work, everyone can count on me, and I fall into bed every night utterly exhausted, but have not love I am nothing. If I keep my body in Olympic shape, make love to my hubby three times a day, and perform marveling acrobatics in the bedroom all the days of my life, but do not have love, I am STILL nothing." Any of those good "wifely" ideals (though extreme) are useless if the wife is resentful, bitter, envious, or angry. But, a woman doing with her heart and is kind, patient, protecting, trusting, hoping, persevering, and rejoicing, that is a beautiful picture. She brings God great joy. Hopefully, it is clear that I am not expecting you to do these particular activities, but whatever you do in your marriage, infuse it with love.

Write in your Workbook #14. Sometimes I imagine in the midst of my actions, Jesus looks at my attitude or intentions and asks "where is your love?" It is a sobering thought. When you think about the end of your life and standing before your glorious Creator, what are the things in your marriage, or posture of your heart that will matter most? Which areas do you see needs work? What areas deserves more of your attention now?

Steamy To Dos:

Spend time talking to your husband about your new views on sex and God's purposes for it. End the conversation with a playful smile and tender kiss. See where else it goes.

SECTION III
Love Yourself

Your Real Heart

We have explored where you are now in your marriage, God's designs and purposes for sexual intimacy, and your choice to be proactive in love. This next section explores how loving yourself is the first step in loving your husband intimately. Jesus said "You shall love your neighbor as yourself." (Matt 22:39). To live this command begins with loving ourselves. The reality is, we often talk to ourselves with cutting, self-deprecating, and critical judgments and that's on a good day. These things we would never dream of saying to another person. When life's heat gets turned up, as it inevitably does, eventually the poison we've been feeding to our own soul bubbles out onto someone else. Instead it's our job to be feeding our souls the kindness and love God has for us. That love and kindness is then what will pour onto others by default. It starts with our own hearts. It will require looking deep inside yourself to recognize where God wants to change your heart. Through this journey, God may take you places in your heart and experience things you never dreamed to be part of physical intimacy. I encourage you to remain curious about what God may teach you about yourself and about loving yourself.

Why Don't You Love Sex?

If sex has been a point of difficulty for you so far in your marriage, it is vital to uncover the reasons. Why do you not *love* the act? When your husband wants to start something and you cool it down, what are the thoughts going through your mind? Self-criticism, memories, physical discomfort, feelings of inadequacy about sexual knowledge, and self-consciousness about body, are all possible barriers.

Write in your Workbook #15 all the reservations or issues that come to mind when you think of making love to your husband.

Read over your list. Become really curious about why these hang ups are continuing to inhibit you. As we dive into some of the issues women have preventing freedom in sexual intimacy, consider where you relate. Think through what areas you need to give to God and seek Him for fresh perspectives.

Sex Is Vulnerable

Marital intimacy requires you to be vulnerable. My guess is you don't like vulnerability, like every other person on earth. It's messy, scary, uncomfortable, and it makes you feel out of control so many times. It is inherently risky. You risk feeling foolish, you open yourself up to ridicule and criticism. You open yourself to danger. I hear you. And almost nothing dredges up vulnerability like physical intimacy. It is easy for me to shed tears in this area with my husband--nowadays more good/healing tears than hurtful/bad--but intense emotions either way. Vulnerability is inherently close to our hearts, it is in fact uncovering and exposing our true selves to another. In order to truly know your husband and to be known by him, in the bedroom and in every other part of your marriage, the walls that normally are healthy to separate and guard ourselves, must be brought low.

Unfortunately, life has taught us that being vulnerable can get us hurt. In grade school, maybe you told a friend the name of your secret crush and she blabbed it to the whole school. Or your high school sweetheart dumped you right when your life seemed to be falling apart around you. Or after you told your college boyfriend you loved him, you found out he was cheating. These were *painful*. Your tender, trusting heart was crushed. You learned it is not worth the risk. You grew up adding guards around your heart to protect yourself. It is natural and often healthy to establish protection from such hurt. But, it is possible these areas of your heart do not recognize where you are in your life now. You're in a loving marriage. The potential hurt you're trying to avoid from your past should not be present any more. I am not advocating you throw caution to the wind if you are not in a safe marriage. There are situations which boundaries in place do protect in the midst of an unhealthy marital season (a great resource on this topic is Boundaries in Marriage by Townsend and Cloud). Assess your marriage and find out if there are areas in which your guard needs to be taken down.

In her book Daring Greatly, Brene Brown elucidates the necessity of vulnerability for true, deep connection with anyone. When you think of someone in your life who allows herself to be vulnerable (though she feels all of those uncomfortable vulnerable feelings in the moment) she looks courageous [1]. It takes courage to show your messy feelings even when they can't be tied up in a nice, put-together package. It takes courage to stand before your husband who hurt you and say calmly and respectfully that you were wounded by what he said. It takes courage to admit that you were wrong and ask for his forgiveness. It takes courage to have a raw conversation with him to tell him you'd like to try some new things in bed and you'd like his help. It takes courage to walk into the room scantily clad in front of your husband and trust he will love it. It takes courage to initiate lovemaking. It takes courage to let your guard down and experience orgasm. It takes courage to bring up difficult bedroom conversations. It takes courage to be vulnerable in sex.

Write in your Workbook #16. When and in what ways do you feel most vulnerable in the bedroom?

Intimacy Requires Vulnerability

I bet you wish you didn't have to be vulnerable to achieve sexual bliss in your marriage. Sometimes, I do too. Vulnerability is hard and often painful. Without true vulnerability, however, there can not be *true* intimacy. It may be possible to have an exciting (short-lived) fling without the discomfort of vulnerability. To have a deep, true, and fulfilling connection with your husband, vulnerability is necessary. Vulnerability means unprotected or unguarded. Here's a visual that helps my understanding of vulnerability in intimacy. Imagine you and your husband are suited up in full medieval armor, complete with helmets, swords, and shields. Can you imagine trying to have physical intimacy with the armor on? Even giving each other a hug just wouldn't be comfortable (if possible) and at the very least it wouldn't be a satisfying hug. What if your husband takes off his armor and is vulnerable to you, but you keep yours on? You more than likely would hurt him with your armor, sword, or shield in an embrace. It is not possible to truly support him without letting down your own guard too and take off your armor. Imagine after years of this armor separating, you two slowly take off the armor and move towards each other in embrace. What a wonderful and full feeling comes from such an embrace. This is the picture of true intimacy, through vulnerability. God set it up this way.

Our Model Of Vulnerability

If this vulnerability thing seems too hard and not worth your risk, I'd like you to consider the best example of vulnerability: God. He models vulnerability. He is completely higher and other and worthy and beyond comprehension in perfect holiness. Yet have you ever considered how vulnerable this unfathomably incredible God makes Himself to *us*? He takes the first step with no guarantee that it will be received or appreciated (or honored and glorified as He deserves). Actually, He goes far, far beyond the first step. His vulnerability is huge. "He chose us in Him before the foundation of the world" (1Pet 1:4). He designed, fashioned, and dreamed of a purposeful life and calling for you and me, before you were even born. His vulnerability goes much farther. He loved you so much that His son came to earth, lived a perfect life, and sacrificed Himself for you and me. There was no guarantee we would even acknowledge this gift and come to Him. All so that He could have a relationship with you and me. *That* is vulnerability. Can you imagine the heart He has for every human to be in a relationship with Him? Imagine the immense heartache He experiences because of those who reject Him. God knew there was risk all along. He knew when He chose to create and love humans. Thankfully, He decided the potential reward of us loving Him was worth His risk. So, when God asks you to "love your neighbor as yourself", or "love your husband, even though..." He understands the risk of vulnerability. He understands and asks you to take that risk.

After tiptoeing around an issue for days between D and I, I have learned to recognize that there is something there. I try to think through *what* is there and how I feel about it. After identifying clearly, I try to address it calmly, gently and graciously. I try also to explain my own honest *feelings* about it instead of jumping to accusations. When I share my feelings, I'm being vulnerable. By modelling vulnerability it provides a safe space for *him* to also respond in vulnerability. Often I'll have tears streaming down my face through it (sometimes I'm not the only one). After a heartfelt conversation, it feels like the wall that before had been separating us, was lifted. Life can be truly be beautiful after the storm-cloud feelings dissipate. You may be surprised that because you courageously went into the storm, a whole new level of connection between the two of you has now opened. Work at leaning into the discomfort, allow yourself to put down your armor, and reap the rewards of that labor.

Write in your Workbook #17. How do you see your views on vulnerability changing? How is vulnerability valuable in your marriage? How can you be more vulnerable in your marriage and intimacy?

Your Feelings Are Valid

A part of loving yourself is acknowledging the value of your feelings. Your emotions often run deep. They are pointing to something that God may want to heal, change, improve, love on, allow you to move on, forgive, give you understanding about or just experience. I have trouble in this area.

As many of you know, I grew up with some dysfunction in my family. My father struggled with alcoholism and my mother was also raised with some dysfunction in her family life. I learned some damaging things about my feelings. Recently, at a support group meeting for families of alcoholics, Alanon, the leader put it very well. "Alcoholism in our family teaches us not to value our own feelings or the feelings of others". This is true of many other family dynamics or life events--not just alcoholism. Put another way, 'if we undervalue our own feelings, we cannot value the feelings others'. We need to realize our feelings have value.

Just because we feel something messy does not mean we're "crazy". I dislike when people give that excuse for their emotions or perceptions. As women, we need to lose the excuse "crazy" and delete it from our vocabulary.

Calling yourself crazy is undervaluing yourself as a person and God doesn't like that. He set you up with amazing reasoning capabilities, as well as often unexplainable sensitivities. Yet, if you're struggling with an emotion, others are too and God may have planned that you will one day help them. Calling yourself crazy or discounting your feelings in some other way is damaging. You are not crazy when you have uncomfortable feelings. Instead, you have a feeling that is worth your attention, though it is vulnerable and messy.

Your feelings are valid. Many women are under the impression that ignoring or pushing aside their feelings will make them go away or make them a more desirable mate. Choosing to not indulge in a feeling is sometimes the wisest choice, only if they have been properly processed first. By allowing yourself to feel your feelings, you are able to consider what meaning it is bringing to you. Acknowledging and owning your emotions is treating your full self with value.

Responding Healthily To Feelings

Do not discount your feelings; they are markers to tell you something. Taking responsibility of your feelings and being able to calmly consider their meaning can bring you insight into your heart, your husband's heart, and the current situation. After feeling and considering the meaning behind the emotion, you can present them to your spouse honestly.

Let's look at a practical example in the context of the marital relationship. Let's say I come home and greet my husband with a warm hug and kiss when I walk in the door. He doesn't even acknowledge my presence, that could hurt. Let's say in that moment, I felt like he didn't care about me. There are many ways I could choose to respond.

First unhealthily:

1a) I get very angry and immediately accuse him of being uncaring and rude.

1b) I am quietly offended and avoid him for the rest of the night, fuming with anger.

1c) I am hurt, but move my mind onto other things, so I don't have to deal with a confrontation.

Now let's look at some healthier ways of owning and processing my emotion in the situation:

Option 2a) I feel hurt. I recognize this feeling and think through what was causing hurt. I realize it had been a long, discouraging day for me and I was looking forward to my husband's embrace to assuage my weariness. In reflection, I recognize that had the timing been different, I wouldn't have been so hurt by these same actions. I then calmly and respectfully ask him if we can chat. I explain how I was feeling and that his response made me feel like he didn't care about me being home. Then, I just calmly and sincerely ask him if he felt like he didn't care about me, or if there was another reason he didn't acknowledge my embrace. Then I ask him for a hug and kiss. This ownership of my feelings gets to the heart of what is going on inside of me. It is vulnerable. I am opening my heart up to him and the truth of what is going on inside of me. This gives him an opportunity to understand how his actions really affect me (instead of assuming there was nothing wrong with ignoring my entrance). Because I was honest, vulnerable, and calm, he is able to respond in kind.

Because of my earnest approach...

-He won't feel defensive and can respond with vulnerability as well. He can apologize and give me a big hug, making my day much better.

-Or I may discover he was acting that way because of something I did that really hurt him earlier. It may be my time to apologize so we both can move forward in deeper connection and understanding.

-Or maybe I find out he was having a really stressful day because of bad news he received at work. Had I not asked him in a kind way, I may never have found out. I may have missed the opportunity to support him in his time of need.

Had I ignored my own feelings, I wouldn't have been able to deepen our relationship and connection in any of these ways.

Option 2b) I think through my emotions and realize I felt hurt because it seemed like he didn't even care that I came home. I think about our marriage and realize he does care about me and it really does matter to him that I came home. Then I consider other the possible reasons he may have for not acknowledging my presence. Then I remember he was cramming for work and he only had another half hour for which to study before he had a conference call on the material. So, I decide not to approach him and completely forgive him and let him continue studying. After his conference call, I ask him for a hug and I tell him I'm proud of his hard work on the work project.

Interpreting Your Feelings

In Options 2a and 2b I felt the feeling. I recognized it was a valid emotion and deserved my attention. Upon calm review, I could decide whether or not it also warranted his attention. Then, prayerfully, I could consider a course of action. Feelings have a tendency to grow into a big problem in our hearts if we do not acknowledge and deal with them head on. It is wisdom to accept your feelings and honestly work through them.

> Process the feeling by:
> A) Feel the feeling,
> B) Consider the multiple possible meanings,
> C) Prayerfully determine a calm way to move forward.

Not every feeling is correct. But every feeling provides valuable information and deserves your attention. Maybe it is rooted in some past pain that God wants to heal. It may need to be curtailed with wisdom because you realize the feeling is false or not worth your time. But if you just ignore the feeling without processing the feeling, it will stay with you and come back later in a worse way. In the same way that if you immediately react because of a feeling without processing it, you can cause immense harm to your marriage. Even your uncomfortable feelings about the bedroom should be acknowledged by you. Accept the feeling as having many possible meanings or reasons. It may even be telling you that you need to apply a biblical truth to that feeling.

Moving Through Vulnerability In Sex

Vulnerability in the bedroom feels similar to vulnerability outside. It's funny how God made sex to be such a great analogy to so much of life. We put on our emotional clothes, makeup and cover up any pain or hurt. We go out into the world guarded and protected. But when we're alone with our husband, it is our opportunity to remove the cover ups, take off the clothes, and be our true selves. I realize going without clothes in front of your husband does not feel good at first. It may take a while for you to feel truly relaxed being bare-bottomed in front of your honey. As you keep at it, feeling comfortable in the vulnerability of your nakedness will support your marriage in a meaningful way. I don't mean you should always be nude around the house. I do mean getting to a place of confidence when you are nude or scantily-clad in front of him frequently. Generally, it is more exciting for him to be used to seeing you in clothes, but to wear much less or nothing at all to give him a visual feast.

I had to do some soul searching when I realized, though I have some sexy lingerie and teddies in my drawer, I was rarely bringing them out for the pleasure of my husband. I came to realize that I was running from vulnerability. Nowadays, when I sense that, I know I need to resist running from it and instead lean into the vulnerability, only then can I uncover what is really going on.

Seek to Understand the Discomfort

I searched my feelings and realized I am not wearing these sexy things (sexy things I know bring my husband great pleasure) to protect myself. Let's say I am naked to seduce my husband. If he shows that he's not in the mood, I could pretend I was just changing, it's too hot, or I am just trying to be comfortable. Being naked, I am less open to being rejected. When I am wearing sexy lingerie, my intention to seduce my husband is very clear. For heaven's sake, I'm not wearing them to be comfortable. By wearing my sexy outfit and giving him a show, I'm asking "Do you find me attractive? Do you think I'm sexy? Do you desire me? Am I beautiful to you?" All very vulnerable questions. I was avoiding them because I wasn't confident the answer would be "Yes!" When I made the decision to press into these vulnerabilities and go for it, the fears dissipated. He did really enjoy my more sexy outfits. He gave greatly positive responses to my advances.

I'd encourage you to lean into the discomfort of vulnerability. Let those difficult feelings wash over you, do not run from them. Seek out what they are telling you. The waterfall of discomfort cannot kill you. Push into them until you get to the other side. Recognize it may not feel good for a couple of moments, but you are setting the stage for deeper intimacy that cannot be achieved otherwise. And your husband will love your sexy panties.

Write in your Workbook #18. What vulnerable feelings are you running from? How can you feel them, understand them, and possibly press into them?

Steamy To Do:

Wear an especially sexy outfit in front of your husband. Let yourself feel the discomfort and press through it. You'll be ok. I bet you'll thank me later.

Moving Through the Pain

The Pain in Intimacy

I know a lot of this may sound difficult for you and I want to address that. There are marriages that are on difficult times right now for very valid reasons. Infidelity or a tragic loss may have brought your marriage to its knees. A pattern of constant criticism may have wrought destruction on your confidence. Maybe reading through some of my examples of a wonderful marriage has reminded you of how painful the place of intimacy has become. You may feel that your husband isn't the man you fell in love with. Beloved, I am so sorry for this intense pain. They are such deep heart wounds. Acknowledging this pain is not an easy task. It is important for you to go into your heart and find out why things have gotten to their current state.

Write in your Workbook #19. Describe any pain or discomfort you feel around the sexual experience with your husband. Are there specific experiences that have caused these feelings?

Your Move

Without knowing your answers, I realize that your pain is real. And it may be rooted in *very* difficult experiences. It may be very valid feelings of sadness or disappointment. You may have been wronged. You may have made painful mistakes yourself. Whatever your circumstance, I do not write these next paragraphs with flippancy. Your pain is real. At this point, reading this book, you are ready for action. Wherever your marriage is now, you have a handful of options.

1) Give up. I gave up on my first marriage. I mentioned this. It was a very bad situation. Though I know God intends marriage to be a bond of lifelong unity, I feel God delivered me from that situation and I give Him glory for it. That was my experience and there are mistakes I had to repent for before the Lord as well. I do hope you're not at the level of brokenness that we were. But if this is something that has been on your mind, try some things before moving to file papers. Your marriage is worth trying some avenues for redemption. I would strongly suggest the following. a) Engage in Christian marital counseling together to work through the issues. b) Seek counsel from your pastor and church mentors who can direct you in this area. Be very open and honest with what is truly going on in your heart and the marriage. c) Depending on where things are, it may be wise to reside in separate physical spaces for a season (separate houses) with counseling and other support in place. d) Pray and meditate on scripture. God longs to speak to you and bring healing to your heart in the midst of the storm.

2) Hold onto the pain and keep dredging through. This is my least favorite option. At least with the first option, you're being honest with yourself, you're taking stock of what is really going on, and you have a plan that can move things in a better direction. But holding onto the pain ensures each party remains miserable. It practically ensures divorce long term.

My parents both vowed to stay together for different reasons. My mom hated divorce for biblical reasons and no one in her bloodline had ever gotten divorced. My father's parents went through a horrible divorce when he was a kid and left all involved bitter and terribly wounded. That was the backdrop of my parents' marriage. I know for some years my parents were happy and enjoyed each other. Slowly the small issues built into very large ones. My father began abusing alcohol to a greater degree and my mom was pained by his lack of engagement and dependability. He wounded her deeply and she did the same to him. One key problem was neither were able to get past the hurt caused by each other. There was always tension because of the pain that happened before. (There is a fantastic book called Boundaries by Dr. Henry Cloud and Dr. John Townsend which is well-worth reading if you are facing any similar troubles). This happens in many marriages. The couple never takes steps to take responsibility for their own actions and apologize and change when they should. They never are truly vulnerable and talk about how they feel. I don't blame them for lack of vulnerability. So often, there is no safe space for this. Since couples vow to stay together, it sometimes provides a false sense of security, assuming it could never break. So both parties feel confined and emboldened to hurt each other since the other had to take it. Thinking they were fighting *for* their marriage, they were wounding each other instead. Even years after their divorce, it is still sad to see the remnants of the damage they caused each other.

3) Forgiveness. Do note that anything you are not intentionally cultivating is in the process of dying. This is true of your marriage, your relationship with God, your friendships, your business...anything in your life. Dear sister, please realize your marriage is a gift from God. You are responsible (just as your husband is) to tend to this relationship. It is your responsibility to nurture and protect it, to feed and water it. Do not think for a moment that this will happen on its own. You have to be the one who takes action. You probably will have to do it before your husband does. You need to model maturity, love, vulnerability, and forgiveness. When asked how many times we are to forgive others, Jesus replied "I tell you, not seven times, but seventy times seven."

(Matt 18:22). Now if our husbands receive 490 forgiveness passes, we had better get pretty good at it. God asks us to forgive others the same way Jesus forgave us and *doesn't even remember* the wrong we did. When was the last time you forgave your husband like the holy, perfect, King of Glory completely forgave you? Are there things you are holding against your husband? Are there areas that you have held a grudge voiced or unvoiced?

In your Workbook #20. Write down each area of your marriage in which you need to forgive your husband. Write everything you can think of. Anything you have held against him that you still feel angry or sad about, even as far back as your dating relationship. Read through each item. Ask God to give you the strength and grace to forgive your husband of every item. Completely.

Pray with me: *Lord, I remember your immense forgiveness and mercy you have shown towards me. Thank you for forgiving and loving me even though I have deeply hurt and wronged you. In the same way, I forgive my husband for...[insert]... I ask you God to help me to walk in this forgiveness every day. Cause me to not meditate or let myself remember these wrongs. In Jesus' name. Amen.*

Cover Over Sin

I'm glad you thoroughly captured the things you've been holding against him and now have released them to God. That will have to become a daily practice to really walk in forgiveness. You are not to take back these items. Can you imagine if Jesus took back His forgiveness? He will not and you should not. "Forgive as the Lord forgave you" (Col 3:13). If you find yourself bringing something up to your girlfriends or getting angry over something you have forgiven, simply tell God: *I forgive him the way You forgive me. Help me to fully forgive him. I release this to You.* Forgiveness starts in the heart, but it also affects our outward actions. It means overlooking someone's wrongs. It means laughing at a joke that could have offended you based on the past. It means pressing reset on a relationship. It means biting your tongue and giving him grace.

The Bible tells us "Above all, love each other deeply, because love covers over a multitude of sins." (1 Pet 4:8). That means you "cover over" or hide your husband's sin. You protect him from others' judgment. You are the last place the sin is seen or heard. Because you *love* your husband, you will protect his reputation before others. Because you love your husband, you will cover over his sin and not bear it to the world. Because you love him and love "keeps no record of wrongs" (1 Cor 13:5). Because God forgave you and sees you as fresh, clean, and holy, you are able to walk with your head held high. Give your husband this gift. Forgive him and forget the wrongs. Let him walk with his chest out and his head held high, knowing that you see him clean and forgiven just as God does. If it would be encouraging to him, you may need to tell him you have fully forgiven him. You may also need to apologize for the ways you held a sin over his head.

Instead call him "an honorable man" and "a man who has your respect". Tell him all the things you notice and love about him. Be generous in your praise. Give him a positive identity to uphold. Tell him how proud you are of him. Tell him how grateful you are for him. Change your thinking. Notice and tell him of his strengths. Be glad you have the husband you do for the purposes God has planned for you both together. Make the decision and change.

Write in your Workbook #21. What changes are you going to make immediately in your marriage?

Steamy To Do:

As you are ending a positive phone call with your hubby, give him a very warm and sincere compliment. Then, just before your obligatory "I love you", insert some spice. Find your sexy and confident voice and say "I can't wait to get you in bed tonight. Love you. Bye." Hang up before he can respond. I guarantee he'll be smiling.

Sexual Wholeness

Our Sexual Journeys

Now that you have bravely worked through a lot of the heart stuff, the next step of wholeness is understanding yourself and the practicalities of your sexuality. We touched on this in the last section, but let's go deeper. Understanding your sexual journey will give you insights to the way you think and allow you to be free from them.

Part 1: My Ignorance

I'll give you some of the highlights of my journey. As a young adult, I was very unaware of my own body. To discourage interest, my mom would give negative facial expressions about private parts and curiosity around them. I'm sure she didn't intend to have a negative effect on my sexual confidence later in life. My young heart thought her silence means that my body is not desirable. I think her only aim was to stave off my sexuality for as long as possible. I guess it worked. I basically never even came close to losing my virginity until I was a young bride.

My father was very busy between many kids, a consuming construction business, and his struggle with alcoholism. I grew up trying to please him and gain his attention and approval. I had to stay quiet in order to stay in the workshop, watch him work with power tools, and listen to country music on the radio. I worked hard to gain his approval. I also tried to keep a stiff upper lip wrestling with my older brother, so he'd think I was a worthy playmate. It worked until his real friends came over and then I was clearly unwelcome.

These experiences taught me to be extremely nervous around boys growing up. I wanted to have friends at school that were boys, but I never could feel comfortable around them. I would quickly get a crush on just about anyone who gave me attention, even as a friend. I could feel my face turning apple red if a boy looked in my direction. I was very active in our church youth group which was a great asset to my self-esteem and walk with God. I heard a lot about how we should wait until getting married to have sex. I was all about it. My young heart interpreted this value as worthwhile because of my low self esteem. I couldn't understand why anyone would want to do this thing with undesirable me. I longed to be married because once someone was committed to me for life, they'd see my gross body on our wedding night and it'd be too late for them to run away.

Part 2: The Hurt

I succeeded in not having sex until I was married. I happened to marry the first guy who had the guts to tell me I was beautiful, clearly desired me physically, and wanted to marry me. He was much older and I had *no clue* how valuable and precious my body or sexuality were. I was very unconfident and naive. Though I wasn't as eager to marry as he was, the fact that he insinuated this desire early on was flattering to me. It caused me to feel that maybe this was a way out of my insecurity and desperation to be loved. He was a strong Christian but I believe was caught in a lot of hard realities inducing untold amounts of stress which affected his mental health.

As I found out, he was not happy that I was a virgin. He insinuated that it was my fault that I couldn't orgasm, give him pleasure, or even understand how a woman *should* enjoy sex. These caused my heart untold hurt and sadness. It was incredibly painful and left me crying myself to sleep often. After a long process, I have been able to truly forgive him. It gave me an insatiable desire to understand sex in all the ways I was lacking; I took courses, classes, read books, blogs and listened to podcasts. "And we know that in all things God works for the good of those who love him, who have been called according to his purpose." (Rom 8:28). As a side note, I should mention that I am grateful for these difficult experiences. I learned through all of them. I learned that keeping a young woman ignorant of her sexuality is not protecting her; it is inhibiting her and leaving her susceptible to the world. The Bible tells us not to be ignorant of the devil and his schemes (2 Cor 2:11). I have learned that I will not let my children loose in the world unaware of their worth as a person and marriage partner, of the true sexual realities in life, and their value as a sexual being.

Part 3: My Rebellion

After my marriage ended, I was angry at God and couldn't understand why He brought me to a marriage that would leave me so broken and pained. I came to understand sex as power. It wasn't special or intimate. It was a form of power. I did not have that power in my marriage and suffered many rejections and feelings of inadequacy. But then I realized I could be a desired seducer. I could be confident and sexy. I started reading books on sexual prowess. I turned to the secular world to educate me even more. I learned a lot and, sadly, I practiced them outside the bounds of marriage. Regrettably, I was used to flings and hookups at that point. I was used to using my sexuality as a short ego trip and adrenaline rush. I just wanted to feel desired and beautiful. I wouldn't stay around long enough to let my heart get too involved so I wouldn't have to risk being hurt again. I was fearless--or so I thought. In the midst of my "sexual freedom", I was suffering from an eating disorder, not paying my bills, and I was mostly void of close friendships. I didn't want anyone to hold me accountable for my recklessness. I had been hurt and now it was my turn to have power. Little did I know that I was wounding my heart in ways that I would later deeply regret.

Part 4: God's Kindness

D was different. Something about him was calming. On our first date, I never wanted the night to end--which was unusual for my independent ego. He was kind. He was patient. Though I didn't give him much reason to, I could tell he respected and honored me. He let his heart be open to my (unsafe) heart. Shortly after we were dating, I remember we were at breakfast in a cute brunch joint. Our conversation turned to my past and I felt overwhelmed with D's deep value and care for me and my feelings. Sitting across from him, warm tears began streaming down my face. He valued my worth as a woman, not as a sexual object.

Even now, I'm tearing up remembering the way he so confidently and kindly cut through my pain and showed how truly he cared for my heart. Unfortunately, I was such a wounded woman and as often happens, "hurt people hurt people". We had our share of difficulties, but D proved to me he would not let me go. He said he would fight for me, and he did. Even when I resisted, struggled, and hurt him deeply. He was pained. But thank God (!) he did not give up. Slowly, slowly my calloused heart began to feel again. I realized true love and vulnerability was not for the naive, but for the courageous. It took courage to let this man into my heart and bare my soul to him and all it's terrible imperfections. I fell deeply in love with D.

Part 5: Healing

I viewed sex as a weapon, not as something to be honored and valued. D helped me to understand what sex was meant to be. I was wrought with insecurities and I was guarded--I had masked them as my mystery. I had never been able to physically enjoy sex. It was an act and it had always been about the other person. I enjoyed the adrenaline rush and flattery leading up, but there wasn't much more than that. I never had an orgasm in my life and was very unaware of how my body responded sexually. While with D, I read a book which helped me to explore my body and the ways I got turned on [4]. Sometimes, I would read D a chapter and ask him what he thought about it. I remember once asking D to tell me what parts of my body he liked.

To my shock (which of course brought many tears), he described the very shameful areas that I felt were dirty and undesirable all my life. Areas I had wished for liposuction, plastic surgery, or wished for others' perfection. It took a long time for me to understand that he was truly and deeply appreciative of these areas that had been sources of my deep shame. My clothes started to be more modest as I began to recognize just how attractive my features really were. My husband began to be more open with me about my beauty and I realized I didn't want other men to desire me in that way and covered up more. I began to feel sexy, vulnerable, and loved in our relationship. I orgasmed for the first time with him. Then I began regularly orgasming multiple times during lovemaking. It has grown from there. I am continuing to grow in my sexual wholeness and freedom from so many hurts and pains the enemy caused me over the years.

Write in your Workbook #22. That's my journey of sexual understanding, growth, and healing. What is yours? Have you ever articulated it fully? What did you believe about your body as a kid? Why did you feel this way? What has been your progression of sexual understanding? Are there areas of your body that are still an area of shame?

Know Yourself

I hope you were pretty verbose with your sexual journey, like I was. I encourage you to be as thorough as possible on this area. What really happened in your childhood to make you feel the way you do about your body? About your sexuality? I was blessed to have my husband help me to recognize my value. You may not have a man that has these particular strengths to help you in your healing. However, God has purposes for your husband's strengths and D probably lacks in ways that your husband excels. God wants you to be healed in every part of your sexuality. He made your body and loves every part. He desires you to see yourself as valuable. He designed every inch as good and wonderful. God wants you to be whole. He wants to heal every area of your heart and make you free to have the most amazing marriage.

Healing The Hurt

As I mentioned, "hurt people hurt people". My hurt deeply harmed my husband. I caused him indescribable pain at times in our relationship because I was unaware of my brokenness and need for healing. My husband had to work through these and forgive me. I hurt members of my family through cutting words and disengagement. Some of my family relationships are still on the mend because of it. You do not know who you are affecting by living in hurt. Your pain may be undermining your most valued relationships.

Pain is a nasty thing. It makes us self-centered. When we're drowning in self-pity, agony, and selfishness, we cannot be present to others' needs. Without even being cognizant, we lash out and cause harm to those closest to us. God wants you healed--for your benefit and the benefit of those around you. Sexual wounds go deep. People don't talk nearly enough about the need of sexual wholeness. But it is a vital need. In this day and age, most of us have wounds as far back as childhood that still affects us today.

Way For Sexual Wholeness

To find peace and healing in this area, it may take talking through these matters with a trusted girlfriend, your husband, a female church leader or a counselor. I encourage you to pray about who to share your experiences with.

Write in your Workbook #23. Through your sexual journey, identify the places of pain. The places you can see you were harmed, misunderstood your value, and wounded your heart.

Pray: *Lord, I ask you for your healing touch. God, would you show me truth in the areas that the enemy has lied and hurt me? Would you heal every part of my heart in the area of sexuality? Help me to run to you in my hurt and show me how much you love every part of my body and how valuable I am as your daughter.*

Spend Time With The Healer

Spend time with God. Let Him heal you. Practically speaking, your time with Him could look like fifteen minutes, sitting in a quiet place listening to worship music. Out loud tell God about these hurts. Describe to Him your pain. Tell Him how you feel about these situations. Ask Him to come. Ask Him to work in these areas. Ask Him to heal you. To strengthen your heart. To give you wisdom and power on the inside when a situation like this happens again. Speak scriptures out loud that help you to get truth in your heart. Meditate on these scriptures: speak them, read them, write them, pray them, and even sing the scriptures. Pray these verses over yourself. Ask God to show you how and give you grace to live these truths. Give Him time to meet you where you are. Remind your heart that He is your loving Father, Comforter, and Friend. He values your every part and hates that people have harmed you. He *loves* you. He enjoys you. He delights in you. Do this once for fifteen minutes (feel free to set a timer) one day. Then do it again and again in the days following. Keep at it--God is faithful to meet your faith and give you true wholeness.

Pray with me: *Lord I ask you to heal me completely. Show me how you feel about these experiences. Show me how you love me so deeply and truly. Show me how you love my body and designed it as completely beautiful. Help me to enter into this process of healing and bring me to sexual wholeness. In Jesus name, amen.*

As you grow and heal, be patient with yourself. It is a process. I am such an action-oriented person it makes me anxious to hear anything "will take time". But God wants to be present and partner with you in your healing. He can bring us to wholeness in many different ways. For me, He used time with Him (as described above), trusted girlfriends, openness with my husband, mentors, books, journaling, audios, and my own reflections through daily life. Meditate on God's truth in the scriptures. Let God redefine your view of sex, your body, and your marriage. Agree that your body is designed divinely and beautifully. You do not have "trouble areas". You are not "damaged goods". You are forgiven and free. Agree that God loves every inch of you and He made every area on purpose. Dig into the pain with grace and mercy for yourself and God's truth.

Steamy To Do:

Ask your husband to tell you what he loves about your body. Let him know you'd like specifics...and you would prefer if he would touch and compliment his favorite parts. Encourage him to take his time.

Confidence Unveiled

How Confidence Is More Sexy Than It Looks

It took me a long time to understand this: your husband will find you more sexy, if *you* find you sexy. Seriously, confidence is sexy. A sexy wife knows her sex appeal. She uses it to seduce and entice her husband. She shows him how much she wants him sexually. He loves that. He wants to feel wanted and when you are confident to go for it, your looks become supercharged for his desire. Think back to your high school prom. If a young man boldly came up to you and respectfully asked you to dance--you'd have been flattered. You probably would have even accepted. But your heart would do no fluttering for the even cuter boy sitting in the corner who does not have the confidence to even say hello. You would ignore him altogether regardless of his looks. You'd find your confident dance partner even more attractive. Confidence is a powerful force.

The most successful people on the planet are the ones that had confidence to go for their dreams and even convince others. They just ignored negativity and pressed on confidently. Whatever tapes you've been playing in your head to make you think you can't be a confident and sexy wife is nonsense. It needs to be changed. You are a brilliant creation and there is no part of you that was designed by mistake. Now people in your past may have clouded your vision of what God designed in you, but it's time to erase those negative messages and rewrite new ones. You can go after what you want and you can achieve it. You can be confident in front of your hubby, regardless of what you're wearing (or not wearing). These are possible and you do not have to be a slave to the lie that you have to first achieve some level of fitness or physical perfection to "earn" this feeling.

Confidence Is a Choice

Confidence is key in the bedroom. I want you to know I understand the feeling of wanting him to do everything, because you're scared or insecure. You don't know if you'll do it right. You don't want him to really see your body, so you stay still and kind of hide.

To be a great lover, you have to break out of your fear. This *is* a choice. You can choose fear or you can choose confidence. If confidence doesn't seem so easy, think about this. When was the last time you rode in a car? Maybe even today? You risked your life more during that drive than you would have bungee-jumping, skydiving, and swimming in shark-infested waters all in the same day. I've heard of grandmothers being scared of cars. Well, Grandma has good reason to be afraid. Auto accidents remain as a leading cause of death in the United States, averaging about 100 per day [2]. But, unlike Grandma, you and I put our attention on other things. She keeps her mind thinking about the accidents and what could go wrong.

How do you drive confidently with all the risk involved? The answer is simple: you would rather drive than walk to the store. You choose to ignore the risk and focus on the destination. Shake off your grandma-self and put on your confident-self. Care more about your dream of a fulfilling marriage than those other nagging concerns. Check your goals in your Workbook from the first section again, and remind yourself "Being confident is worth it". Focus more on your desire to be a great lover. Focus more on the joy you want to bring to the man you will be with forever.

Keep refocusing on that desire. It will take practice. You will need to practice wearing sexy outfits, being naked, kissing and loving on your man physically. You will need to practice leaning into the discomfort of something that is new. But with practice that discomfort will dissipate and confidence will feel more natural. Marriage is the only opportunity in this life to have true intimacy with another person. It requires bravery, but it is worth it.

Ask any woman and she'll probably admit she feels most vulnerable about her body. Ask any man, and he probably feels most vulnerable about his feelings. (He may or may not admit this because that is a deep feeling, thus vulnerable to share). Funny, but aren't we women extremely attracted to our man's feelings and emotions as he slowly opens up? Men feel the same way of their woman's body (even more so!). He longs for you to feel confident and comfortable in your own skin. So confident that you flaunt it and tease him with it.

Notes From Ms. Susan:

You have to take care of yourself through all of your seasons. You really do. Physically. You have to take care of yourself physically. Men are much more visually attracted. They fell in love with you wherever they fell in love with you. So I would say make that your base line. Obviously bodies shift and they change and you have to deal with when your life is very stressful and you don't get enough sleep. When you don't have time to workout or go to the gym. All of those things. Our bodies are going to change. But even as you gain 10 pounds, look nice for him. Go out of your way for him. Not all the time. You don't have to be anyone other than who you are. But make that effort often enough that he sees you as that beautiful woman that he fell in love with.

If you have gained more than 10 pounds, it's not good for you anyway. Really it's just so much better for your marriage to do everything you can to lose it. I think that you can have a conversation about that. I think you can say to your husband, "I know I am really letting myself go here. I just don't have the time. I don't have the energy... I really want to be beautiful for you. Can you help me do this?" A lot of times I see older couples and honestly both of them have let themselves go. Like you said, I see marriages at all stages. But I hear from both parties "I am just not attracted to him anymore. It is really hard for me to have a great passionate sex life because I am not attracted to this person physically. And it's getting in the way".

That is a really hard conversation to have. It is an extremely hard conversation to have when things have gone too far. Because now the person doesn't feel good about the person that they are anyway. So now I'm already 25 or 30 pounds overweight, out of shape, and I don't feel good about myself. Now my husband is telling me "this is really hard for me...". You don't want to go there. Or probably worse yet, he's not telling you at all. It means he may be shutting you out. Why? Because you're not talking about it. So catching those kinds of things early on, and talking it through, figuring it out, making space for each other so that you can stay attracted to each other. It is so important.

Loving Yourself Physically

Our society could not be hammering physical perfection into our heads more than they do already. It is hard to fight the pressure to compare and judge ourselves badly on a physical level. Let's ignore those negative voices and think about it from God's perspective. To love yourself and honor the temple God has given you, being healthy in your food choices and your exercise will let you live a better life. It will let you feel more confident and give you more energy than you can imagine. It will let you thrive in your marital intimacy as well. I don't want to spend much time on this, because I don't want you to get in your head that you cannot be confident without already achieving your goals. But you can make small changes that will have a positive effect on your attitude, energy, and personal feelings of beauty. I should also mention that if Ms. Susan seems a little flippant about the area of weight loss, I should add that she also has worked in the fitness industry since early in her marriage. She has helped hundreds of women shed the unwanted pounds, so she knows it's possible for you too!

Even *one* day of healthy eating or 10 minutes of exercise can make you feel exponentially better in the bedroom that night. Seriously try just *one* day, and feel the difference. Realize there is a bigger purpose to the health of your body than posing in a bikini. God wants you to feel vital and live a long life to fulfill His purposes. It is also important to have a wonderfully fulfilling marriage. Make small changes today to make yourself feel better. Love your physical body in this way.

Steamy JoDo:

Decide on one day this week that you are going to be especially healthy in your food and you are going to up your level or exercise. If you are currently not exercising, go for a scenic walk, but pace yourself at double your normal speed. If you currently exercise regularly, take it up an extra notch. Then observe the difference when you approach your husband for lovemaking.

Faith-Focus vs Fear-Focus

Don't Derive Your Worth From Fading Things

"Woah, woah, woah," you might be thinking. "So you wrote a whole book about sex and you're telling me it doesn't matter?" Well, kind of. I am telling you it is not the most important thing. I want you to focus on sex and get a passionate and intimate marriage so that the rest of your life can be more purposeful. Sex is a wonderful gift, but it should not be the focus of your life. It should be a vital support in your life. Sex is a false idol, which the enemy has glorified in our society. The enemy has lied to women that they have to be beautiful, sexually free, and spontaneous. Many women live in fear of falling outside of these descriptors. The enemy is smart. If he can get us thinking about our fears then he can undermine all the work God wants to do through our lives. As women of faith, the enemy has tricked us into thinking we must be Modest Mary on Sunday morning and Sensual Sandra by Sunday night. If we're neither, well we should just go eat a jelly donut. Just forget about the important work God has destined for your life. If he can make us focus on these ideals, he has successfully distracted us from our God-given assignments.

Where You Derive Your Value

Consider a woman who is unable to use her arms or legs, has a debilitating illness, or recovering from breast cancer. You'd agree she shouldn't be void of purpose because her physical appearance doesn't accord with the world's standards. So, why do you judge yourself that way? You and I need our identity to be wrapped up in being a valued creation of the Most High. We are His daughters. We are not of this world. It is only temporary. Things of this earth will fade away (1 John 2:17). We need to keep our thoughts on the things above. This eternal focus has eternal rewards. If we commit to God's perspectives of ourselves we can remain freed up to focus on what God wants to do through us.

We are going to unpack the fears that may be hindering you, but I want you to keep them in context. These fears may come here and there, but you must let them float on by. These fears are not relevant to your life. We must lean into God's strength and resist the temptation to look at ourselves the way the enemy lies to us. We must stand strong and realize our worth is tied to the One who formed us, saw us, and called us worthy. Not for anything we could do to deserve it. Only because of who He is and that He chose us to love. Your constant hope can only be placed in Jesus. Eventually the storms come and knock over the house built on sand. But, for those who built their house upon The Rock, "the rain fell, and the floods came, and the winds blew and beat on that house, but it did not fall" (Matt 7:24-25).

Write in your Workbook #24. What makes you valuable? What are the most important parts of who you are? Should your value be tied to those things? Where *should* your value come from? Ask God right now to change your heart in these areas. Ask Him to help you change your values and not let them lie in the temporary and fading aspects of this world, but to build your foundation upon the Rock.

Why You Don't Have to Be Scared

Maybe it is strange to admit. But fear is a *huge* barrier to your sexual fulfillment. As women who grew up oblivious, abused, or another less-than-ideal background, we are often scared of many aspects of sex. Women who have slowly witnessed their marriage beds becoming stale, often have insecurity at the root. Fear that you're not good enough in bed; fear of not receiving your husband's approval; fear of showing your 'imperfect' body; fear of not knowing how to please your husband. I have wrestled with all of the above fears and more. These fears are so powerful that many women sink into depression, addiction, and other coping patterns to avoid dealing with them. At the very least, women neglect their intimate relationship with their husbands as a result. This has got to stop. The first step toward change is acknowledging the concern. Admitting that these fears nag you and drive a wedge between you and a fulfilling marriage.

Write in your Workbook #25. The fears of not being good enough in bed, of your husband's judgment, imperfect body, or not knowing what to do sexually can be deep pains for women. Which fears are most difficult for you?

Fear Of Inadequate Physical Beauty

Let's move forward being faith-focused instead of fear-focused. I want to spend time clearing up some of the pain points present in your marriage. The reason feeling un-beautiful is so painful is because the enemy has whispered to you that without physical beauty you are not valuable. This is a lie. The enemy doesn't want you to be a confident, wise, passionate wife for the glory of God. The enemy has lied to women that their worth is based on how beautiful and/or sexual they are. Our culture of sexual perversion tainted by porn and sexual promiscuity has influenced minds in this way. Your worth cannot come from your looks, your sexual prowess, even the opinion your husband has of you. Those things fade and cannot be relied upon. Even if you were blessed with beauty in your youth, you will age and no matter how many surgeries or products you use, wrinkles and sagging skin will take its turn.

The enemy also lies to us saying that you cannot sexually satisfy if you are not physically perfect. That is not true. What does God say of your physical beauty? The Bible says nothing of Eve's physical appearance except that she was naked *and* unashamed. There is no mention of her toned arms, amazingly proportional curves, or thimble-sized waist. She may have had a thick midsection, short legs, and flabby arms, but Adam found her desirable and wonderful. He took delight in her beauty. God designed her looks for Adam's pleasure. His first words when she came on the scene was a poetic song (Gen 2:23). It was not in Adam's consciousness to compare her with some standard of beauty. Theologian, Mark Driscoll, says your spouse is your standard of beauty. He says, God gave Adam a spouse and God gave Eve a spouse [3]. So if Eve was tall, Adam was into tall. If Eve was on the more stocky side, that is was what Adam was into. If Eve was short with cankles, Adam was into those too. The perversion of our society has given rise to an idealized measuring stick by which to define beauty. This "standard of beauty" is a lie.

God has made *you*. He has made you beautiful and wonderful. Your job is to discipline yourself to believe this about yourself and your body. Exercising and eating well certainly help in our self-confident feelings, but recognize if you somehow could achieve a supermodel body type, you would *not* be more worthy of love or value than you are *right now*. Yearning for something that is fading is vanity. Do not waste your energy, effort, time, and especially your *peace* on something that is fading. Don't say to yourself, "I'll sexually please my husband once I..." Instead, say to yourself, "I'm going to satisfy my husband now. Maybe later I'll feel more confident, but I'm going to love and serve my husband *now*". I must warn your level of beauty will not matter in eternity. "The Lord does not look at the things people look at. People look at the outward appearance, but the Lord looks at the heart" (Sam 16:7).

Inner Beauty

Imagine for a second if your worth were not tied to your appearance but truly to your heart and character. Would the fear of not being beautiful matter to you? If you were a chef and someone said "your writing is terrible," would you care? Maybe your writing is bad, maybe it isn't. You don't care because what matters to you is your cooking. In the same way, when we get clear on what matters most to us, the temporary concerns (of our culture or the devil's lies) diminish. I find it refreshing that the Bible has very few mentions of beauty as a good thing. Of course it is another gift to be enjoyed by God. But when it becomes an idol, as it is in our society, we must actively resist the temptation.

Check out a couple of verses that encourage inner beauty and devotion to God far above outward beauty. Proverbs 31:30 says "Charm is deceptive, and beauty is fleeting; but a woman who fears the Lord is to be praised." 1 Peter 3:3-4 "Your beauty should not come from outward adornment...it should be that of your inner self, the unfading beauty of a gentle and quiet spirit, which is of great worth in God's sight." Ezekiel 28:17 "Your heart was proud because of your beauty; you corrupted your wisdom for the sake of your splendor." Lastly, (one of my favorites) Phil 4:8, "Finally, brothers, whatever is true, whatever is honorable, whatever is just, whatever is pure, whatever is lovely, whatever is commendable, if there is any excellence, if there is anything worthy of praise, think about these things." By the grace of God, we should daily renew our mind and conform it to these, God's values.

Write in your Workbook #26. What is most important in your life?

When looking back on your life before you leave this earth, what areas of yourself do you want to be evident? Is it striving and despairing for physical perfection OR living in peace and confidence in God, striving for beauty of your inner self?

Dethrone the Idol of Beauty

To be truly free from the desire for a worldly physical perfection, there are practical things you will need to change. First we need to STOP some things.

-Stop looking in mirrors as you pass them on the elevator, in offices, or in your house. Resist checking yourself out as you walk past reflecting glass on storefronts, in car windows, and bus stops. Glancing at your reflection reminds yourself that your looks *are* most important to you. Every glance at a reflection lets you judge yourself on how you look. Start counting every time you catch yourself in a reflection. By the end of today, you may be surprised your number is in the high double digits. Unexpected right? So, twenty to forty times every day we remind ourselves that looks are vital to our life and happiness. But, how many times today do we remind yourself the value of our inner beauty?

-Stop commenting on others' physical beauty as though it is a judgement on their worth. Of course it is an easy conversation starter (I am absolutely guilty of this). But it reiterates to yourself and the other person, that it is the most important thing. Instead of "Wow you look great. Did you lose weight?" try "You seem so energetic! How are you feeling?" or "Happy you're here. I just love seeing your smiling, friendly self." Beauty compliments are obviously not bad, but check yourself if these are the main compliments coming out of your mouth. Try to vary it up to reflect God's values to your friends and acquaintances, instead of society's.

-Stop assuming strangers are judging your physical beauty. When you see a man looking in your direction give him the benefit of the doubt. Assume he is looking your way because he thinks he recognizes you or you remind him of his sister.

-Stop judging others' worth based on their physical appearance. The Bible makes it clear, beauty is not to be our measuring stick and should not be trusted. Bounce your eyes when they land on a part of someone's body which you would normally name as bad or good. Just don't let your mind go there. Bounce your eyes onto something else immediately to ensure your mind will meditate on something of virtue.

-Stop comparing your looks to others. Similarly, do not let your eyes rest on covers of magazines and advertisements of sexy bodies. Do not let yourself meditate on your looks compared to those of supermodels or other figments of societal beauty. Supermodels have achieved physical beauty and it is a constant preoccupation for them. Are their values yours? Would you give up the follower of Jesus, friend, wife, and (spiritual or physical) motherhood so you can have a temporary societal ideal? Might I add an ideal God says is fleeting, deceitful, and vanity.

Let's START doing the following:
-Start using the temptation to check yourself in the mirror or a passing reflection as an opportunity to remind yourself of your inner beauty. Use it to remind you that you are well-loved by your Creator. Use it to pray for God to develop strong character and the fruits of the Spirit in you. Use it to remind you to pray for other women in your life who are following the idol of physical

perfection. Ask God to make your understanding more like His in this area.

-Start speaking with the sword of the Spirit (Ephesians 6:17) when the devil tries to tempt you with the lie that your worth is in your physical appearance. Commit the verses about your inner beauty mentioned above to memory and speak them to yourself when the temptation comes to believe the lie.

-Start looking for ways friends exhibit the character that God values and begin complimenting others with words such as: generous, kind-hearted, gentle, loving, faithful, joyful, peaceful, patient, good, and self-controlled.

-Start noticing the parts of your inner beauty that God has already matured. Develop confidence in your character and the personality traits that God says are wonderful. Thank God that He is growing such wonderful, beautiful parts of your heart day by day.

-Start meditating on "whatever is true, whatever is honorable, whatever is just, whatever is pure, whatever is lovely, whatever is commendable, if there is any excellence, if there is anything worthy of praise, think about these things" (Phil 4:8). Redirect your thoughts when you realize they are contemplating wrong things.

It is time to put this false idol of physical perfection to death. It is time to rid yourself from believing the lie that your physical appearance produces your value. This must be a daily practice of "taking your thoughts captive to make it obedient to Christ" (2 Cor 10:5). You have to rewrite the mental scripts that has become habit. Do not let the mirror define your worth. You must take these thoughts captive, moment by moment. Pray. And trust that you are able to use the power of God to be free of this worldly ideal. Know that "the weapons we fight with are not the weapons of the world. On the contrary, they have divine power to demolish strongholds" (2 Cor 10:4). By the power of Jesus, He will change your heart and mind. Select a scripture to recite when you feel yourself falling into that pit. Spend time memorizing these verses, and when tempted to misplace your worth, *use* the sword of the Spirit (which is the Word of God. Jesus combated the devil by quoting scripture when he was tempted in the desert and you should do the same.

"The world and its desires pass away, but whoever does the will of God lives forever" (1Jn 2:17).

"Set your minds on things above, not on earthly things" (Col 3:2).

"I am fearfully and wonderfully made" (Prov 139:14).

"So we fix our eyes not on what is seen, but on what is unseen, since what is seen is temporary, but what is unseen is eternal" (2 Cor 4:18).

Write in your Workbook #27. Write a prayer to the Lord asking Him to renew your mind. Write the items that you feel convicted in your heart and need to commit to daily walk in God's truth.

Scared of Not Being Good Enough in Bed

I'd like to clarify this fear a bit. Firstly, nervousness about your skill in bed is a *very* common fear. But let's think it through. You love your husband. You chose to be with him instead of any other man on the face of the planet. Yes, maybe you all have already encountered a lot of heartache and hurt each other since that decision, but at some point *you* deemed this man worth giving your life's love to. Now, here you are, scared to give him great pleasure in his most gratifying place.

I wonder if you've ever seen anyone give a speech or presentation who was obviously fearful. Let's pretend a woman named Lisa is giving a presentation to a room full of people. Consider what was likely going through her mind as she is shaking at the podium. Lisa is saying to herself, "Oh gosh, what do these people think of me? I wish I had ironed this shirt once more before leaving the house. I'm not good enough for this presentation. The things I've prepared are kind of stupid anyway. What if they ask me a question I don't know? Maybe they will make fun of me later with their friends. I don't really have anything relevant to say. Why am I even up here?" All Lisa's self-talk is about Lisa. She's focused on herself, her feelings, her nervousness etc. Unfortunately it's a self-fulfilling prophecy in a sense. Her doubts and fears make the presentation not very good, because she is not focused on the purpose of her message or her listeners receiving it. Her nervousness about not being good enough is actually undermining her success.

The best teachers know that they need to meet their students where they are to have most effect in the classroom. A great presenter is completely concerned with what her listeners need to hear and delivering that message the best way possible. But if Lisa's mind is consumed with her own insecurities, she doesn't have any awareness of her purpose in presenting. When we're scared of something involving another person, it's usually because we're only thinking about ourselves. Can you imagine a doctor being too nervous to talk to someone about a treatment that would save his life? But the doctor is just too nervous to share this life saving news. We'd probably all like to scream "Get over yourself--It's not about you". The doctor shouldn't be nervous because his focus should be about his purpose: saving the life of this person. Lisa shouldn't be consumed with herself, instead she should be concerned about her purpose:

meet her audience where they are and teach them what they need.

Nervousness Exposed

In the same way, when we are confronted with the feeling of not being good enough in bed, take the focus off of yourself and onto the purpose of intimacy. Whenever you're feeling nervous about being with your husband intimately, start to think about a) why it is important to have an intimate experience; and b) how you will feel by the end. It seems so simple, but it is *not* automatic. Our fear creeps in and tries to make the experience all about our insecurities. Instead, remind yourself, "Since I want a fulfilling marriage, I am going to enjoy and enter into this experience. What will make this experience great for both of us?" When I start feeling self-conscious, it helps me to begin doing something active for his enjoyment. Being active in the experience helps me to focus my mind and narrow my thoughts on the present.

Hollywood has got it all wrong. In the movies, someone totally consumed with themselves marries the other attractive, selfish person and they live happily ever after. That is not reality. In real life the actual result of the self-centered life is divorce (at the minimum). It is really the generous person who is the best lover. She is confident in herself, because she's consumed with the experience. She is generous and wants to give her husband pleasure.

When he lovingly kisses you and holds you just the way you like it, notice how important his confidence is in your enjoyment. You never have to be nervous about initiating or giving your husband pleasure. Remember, "it's not about you" it is about your marriage. It's about both of you and how this experience adds to the joy and pleasure of intimacy.

Fear is Not Part of Love

Understanding God's truth will set us free from the grip of fear. Begin to flood your mind with the truth of scripture. A powerful verse that is worth committing to memory underscores this point. "There is no fear in love. But perfect love drives out fear, because fear has to do with punishment. The one who fears is not made perfect in love" (1 John 4:18). I have often wondered the meaning and even application of this verse. It's actually only become a core understanding for me recently. It makes so much sense in the context of marriage. Fear is not what God wants for you, ever. He especially does not want it in your marriage. As love becomes greater, fear becomes less.

Whatever your story is, God wants to heal you of your pain. His perfect love for you drives out all fear. As we surrender our fears to God and let his perfect love wash over us, we do not need to be subject to our fears any longer. They do not have to rule over us. God wants husbands and wives to love each other with a deep and enduring love. My prayer is your husband would learn to love you as God does and all fear would be cast out in His perfect love within your marriage.

When you have that love for your husband and he for you, you feel comfortable around him. He is able to be himself. You are able to be yourself. When you are utterly in love with your husband and he you, you cease to fear him. Your loving marriage has no room for fear. You stop craving his approval because you do not fear his disapproval. He can relax in your presence and you in his. That is the marital love God desires for you and fear has no place in it.

Write in your Workbook #28. Are there fears God is prompting you to release to Him? Write out these fears. How do you think God would answer these for you?

Fear is Not God's Plan For You

God references fear over 360 times in the Bible. To sum, they are many different ways of telling us, "do not to fear". Fear is *not* what God wants for you. It says "For the Spirit God gave us does not make us timid, but gives us power, love, and self-discipline." (2 Tim 1:7). The power fear holds over you is not what God intended. He gave you a greater power, the power of the Holy Spirit. Fear of God is the only fear we should hold. Jesus put fear in context when he said, "my friends, do not be afraid of those who kill the body and after that can do no more. Fear Him who, after your body has been killed, has authority to throw you into hell. Yes, I tell you, fear Him" (Luke 12:5). All other fear is the enemy's attacks. God has given you the ability through His Spirit to resist fear and operate in power, love, and a peaceful mind.

As I look at my marriage, and see the love and vulnerability we share, I am amazed at how wonderful marital love can be. It didn't start out that way in our relationship. God has brought it to a place of deep and refreshing waters. D and I were looking at wedding pictures recently and just as the beautiful memories of that day flooded back, it was such a powerful reminder of how grateful we are for each other's love. I am completely in love with my husband and it seems to grow each day.

Write in your Workbook #29. What can you do when you feel fear start to grip you? What truth can you speak to the enemy when he taunts with fears and worry?

Pray with me: *Lord, I present my fears to you. You say I do not have to worry about anything but through prayer and thanksgiving, I can present these to you and your peace will reign in my heart (Phil 4:6). So, God, I ask you for the strength to thank you in the midst of these concerns. I thank you for [insert sincere thanks]. Lord I ask you to change my heart and my husband's heart in these areas. [Insert fears and worries]. Lord I thank you that you are changing my heart to understand and live your truth.*

Steamy To Do:

Determine one action that is normally very scary to do in front of your husband. And do it. Choose to focus on the purpose behind this action; to bring you both together and to become comfortable and confident in intimacy.

Get In Touch With Your Body

Take A Long Shower

I really love taking showers. Hot, steamy winter showers are so wonderful and I refresh with the cool water flowing over my body in summers. After becoming a mother, I let this simple pleasure slip away. It became automatic to take a 10 minute shower to scrub the essentials, put whatever product on my hair, and get out before I was missed. My excess baby weight and my perceived time limitations kept me from connecting to my own body. It started to seem like a foreign place, purposed for scooping up kids, nursing babies, wiping up messes, and working in the moments in between. How could I have time for primping? Where did that appear in my ever growing To Do lists? As the months wore on, I slowly became aware of a vast disconnection.

One day, I was taking a shower and meditating on the way God loves me and how I can gain my sense of wholeness from His love. I turned the temperature to be a little warmer, just how I liked it. I used the loofah to spread suds all over. I spent time intentionally reconnecting and praising God for my body. I started by gently massaging my fingertips then hands, touching each part of my arms. As I worked, I breathed deeply, shut my eyes and thanked God for His holy design. I appreciated Him making this body healthy, strong, beautiful, and capable. I moved up to my shoulders and neck. I spent time allowing the tension to flow out under the pressure of my hands. I spent time acknowledging my uniquely feminine areas. I thanked God for their extraordinary pleasure-providing, life-giving, and intimacy-inducing qualities. I touched and thanked God for my torso and its shape, health, and strength containing so many vital (and incredible) organs. I eventually moved down to my legs thanking God for their stability, vitality, and appeal, massaging the muscles that have faithfully carried me every day. Then moving to my toes, I took extra care to connect with each digit on each toe, massaging the bridge underneath and being grateful that I have had such cute and helpful feet that take me wherever I choose.

Giving myself and God the time to re engage with my physical self gave me a sense of gratefulness and confidence which had eluded me for some time. When I toweled off and came to be with my husband, I entered the room with a new understanding. I felt *precious*. I felt like I understood what God sees in me. By marrying D, I recognized the gift God has given D. God has shared me, my body (His handiwork) with this man to "cherish and hold". My body has great worth.

Part of loving yourself is knowing yourself. It is easy to fall into a rhythm of busyness in life and become out of touch with your body. I would encourage you to do this exercise. Go through line by line and do the same. Re-engage with your senses. Re-engage with God's views of His beloved creation, your body. Spend time acknowledging how precious your body truly is. How magnificent is God's masterpiece. I would encourage you to make this a regular part of your life. Discipline yourself to engage with the amazing gift God gave you when he designed this body for you.

What Turns You On

Giving yourself space to reconnect with your body provides space to understand yourself. Sex is not all about giving to your hubby. I thought that for many years because pleasure was not part of my sexual experience. Each time I engaged in sex, it would be about the other. That caused me to disassociate my unique turn-ons from the act of sex. I had to go through a very intentional process to understand myself and my unique desires. Do you know what your sexual triggers are? As a sensual wife, it is important to embrace your own sexual preferences. You should discover what thoughts, touches, and body parts are arousing for you. This knowledge will help you tune in and turn on when the time is right.

Your hubby loves seeing you turned on. He loves knowing that you want him. A *large* part of his pleasure is seeing you receive pleasure. Spending time figuring out the areas that are sexually gratifying to you is key. There are specific scenes, fantasies, or memories that make you feel tingly. As a God-fearing woman, ensure these mental visuals are about your husband, but otherwise go wild. My husband and I have a reservoir of memories that make me a little hot and stimulated when I call them to mind.

To clarify a large misconception, being turned on is not automatic for most women. Often, we have to be intentional about it. You are unlike your husband in this way. Women generally do not get aroused going through everyday busy life. Every now and then our minds wander in that direction, but it is not as frequent. For many men, even brushing up against a trashcan can provide a jolt of sensation and trigger sexual desires. For us, we need to make the effort to discover ourselves and our sexuality. Let's start this process with the following questions. Dig deep into your memory of experience and become very curious about your unique turn ons.

Write in your Workbook #30. In your workbook, list 5 sexual triggers that gets you revved up and ready to go. List your favorite physical features of your husband's body. What types of foreplay turn you on? Do you enjoy your husband touching your naked body, massaging your back, and gently caressing your breasts? Is there a sexual fantasy about your husband (or one you can create) that gives you desire for sexual pleasure? What other ideas, experiences, stimulation, and visuals get you going? I'd encourage you to try to be as thorough as possible. Really get an understanding of *your* sensuality.

Your Orgasm

I mentioned previously that it was years before I ever experienced orgasm. I know many women are in this preorgasmic stage. Firstly, to be clear, sex is not about orgasm. God did not command sex to start or end because of it. Every stage of the intimate experience you enjoy with your husband is growing your intimacy, pleasure, and unity in your marriage. These are worthwhile purposes of the intimate experience. With that said, before learning to orgasm, I remember assuring myself that I didn't need it. I felt a heightened sense of arousal and by the end of the experience, I felt a sense of satisfaction.

In the back of my mind, there was a nagging sense that I was somehow broken. Why couldn't I get my body to do what it was *supposed* to do? All the expectations of my youth and waiting for sex and I can't even enjoy it? These pressures led to frustration during my intimate times with D. After some honest communication, I felt comfortable that he really wanted me to feel fully sexually free. He did share that he would love to see me enjoy orgasm, but assured me he didn't want me to feel pressured. That helped me to relax. But I remained curious.

I had achieved a level of understanding in the bedroom when it came to his pleasure, but I had not prioritized my own. As I slowly began to understand my value as a woman, I understood sex was not about performance (as the movies would lead you to believe). My own pleasure became more of a priority. I don't think this is a rare scene. The fact that you're drawn to this book, tells me you care about your husband's pleasure. I commend this. However, the reason your pleasure is so vital, is that true intimacy is give and take. You are worthy of sexual pleasure in the bedroom. As an added bonus, your husband receives more pleasure seeing you have pleasure. For most women, clitoral orgasms are the primary way they experience orgasm. Most men (and many women) do not realize this and assume penetration is sufficient.

In She Comes First, Dr. Kerner debunks the myth that women should be able to reach orgasm with male penetration only [5]. He says women and men need to realize the female body will probably not achieve orgasm without specific clitoral stimulation. This is something to be explored. Do not discount the help of a vibrator or your own hand. Your enjoyment in the bedroom is very important. This process of discovery has taken me years. I still have a lot of understanding to uncover. Make no mistake: you are not broken. You are learning your body and how it works. This is an important stage of discovery. Do take the needed time and effort on this. God designed you with the unique ability to orgasm and even enjoy multiple orgasms.

Your Peculiarities

An interesting thing about women that probably eludes your husband is how unpredictable you are. But this is a natural and scientific truth [6]. Women are often turned on in one way today and abhorring it the next. Time of the month, events of the day, your diet, and who knows what else, all influence what things stimulate you at certain times. There are some general things that stay constant, ie light touches around the vulva are much preferred over rough touches to begin. Many things, however, do not stay the same. If you know this to be true about yourself, at least you can come to expect it. As you make new discoveries about yourself, I'd encourage you to let your hubby in on them. You can gently steer him away from something that felt great the day before, either using your hand or a gentle verbal redirection ie: "I'd love for you to...". I'd encourage you to become very curious about what is stimulating to you. Also let this program start you on a journey of sexual exploration, but let it not end here.

If you do not yet orgasm consistently when making love, it only goes up from here! I mentioned that this was not something that came naturally to me (though it does to some). I had to read and explore my sexuality and responses until I reached orgasm for the first time. For me, the pursuit took years. I want you to keep up the hope and apply a little focus to your pursuit. There are quite a lot of good resources for this. Some are included in the resources section. I'll discuss more about communicating new discoveries with your hubby in the next section. I truly believe this pursuit will yield wonderful fruits in your life.

Steamy To Do:

Tell your husband one of your sexual fantasies or steamy memories of you two together. Lying next to him, touching each other, give him every detail of this story. Don't leave out the really intimate parts. You'll both enjoy entering into the experience together.

Prioritize Your Marriage

Most Important Relationship

There should be no human relationship above the relationship with your husband. He is the one to hold you when the world seems cruel and heartless, he'll be there in any medical emergency, he's ½ founder of your family, he's your kids' dad, he is protector of your dreams and heart. If any relationship, besides your relationship with God, is in competition with your marriage you need to seriously reprioritize. Yes, your marriage comes before your kids. As a child to divorce, it is *always* ugly. I was an adult when my parents pulled the plug on a broken marriage after 25 years. Even though I was in college at the time, far removed from the day-to-day hardship for the divorce, it was *devastating*. The depth of hurt that it wrought on both sides has been so sad. God hates divorce. There are many reasons for this. I think it is because He hates heartbreak, he hates separating families, he hates broken promises, he hates selfishness, he hates how it drives people away from His loving embrace, he hates people writhing in pain of slashed dreams and hopes. Many years after my parents' separation, every family function still feels incomplete with at least one parent absent. We're still tiptoeing around how to make sure each grandparent sees their grandchildren enough. So many memories that should provoke belly laughs, instead invoke deep pain and regret. Divorce is awful for wives. If you value your heart, invest *now* in your future happiness by loving your husband and doing the hard work (in counseling if necessary) to get to a good place. Divorce is awful for kids. If you want to love your kids, love your husband *first*.

In my parents' marriage, I did not ever get the feeling that the kids were second to their marriage. I had the freedom to be in every extracurricular activity available. I never took into consideration that my mom would have to drop me off and pick me up from whatever the thing it was. I could basically fill my calendar and mom was the one to make sure it happened. As an adult, I feel grateful for her constant sacrifice. But, as a mom myself I have no earthly idea how she did it. I see how difficult and depleting such a life is for a wife and for a marriage. After a day of running after kids, picking up, dropping off (not to mention tending to, or--more difficult--making us tend to our many pets) how was their energy left for anything else? In retrospect, though I may have whined and pleaded, I would have done well with some limits set and boundaries enforced. I was a *child*. It would have been good for me to know my place in the household every now and then. My major prayer request as a kid was for my father's salvation, his alcoholism, and my parents' marriage. I obviously don't know what would have happened if my mom had set limits and more so prioritized her marriage. It probably was in reaction to hurt she felt and kids were a welcome distraction to that. It's not possible to know what could have happened. I can at least take lessons to avoid in my own child-raising habits.

When I spent a summer working in a country in Africa, I stayed with a wonderful missionary couple. They were clearly in love after 4 children and 23 years of marriage. One morning, I wanted to retrieve a book I had lent to the mother. When she said it was in her bedroom, I proceeded to walk in that direction. She stopped me and clarified that the bedroom was just for she and her husband. She explained that her own adult kids were not permitted. I was surprised but now, looking back, grateful. I learned a significant secret to their long-lasting flame. Seeing them together you could see they were completely head over heels for each other. Respect the bedroom and what happens there. It is a key and vital part to a fulfilling marriage. Let it be a set apart for your marital intimacy and enjoyment. Leave stresses, worries, and family members outside of it.

Relational Priorities

My husband and I have decided to prioritize our relationships in life this way: 1-Relationship with God, 2-Our marriage, 3-Our kids, 4-Everyone else. Your marriage flows into every other part of your life. A fulfilling and fruitful marriage makes for a wonderful life. Spend the time and energy to put your marriage on the right path. I'll tell you a secret, you need to have this in your mind *before* times get bad. Just as your car will carry on well with *regular* attention, namely frequently filling the gas, changing the oil, and giving tune ups. Once you've missed enough times of this vital maintenance, the car is actually time bomb on wheels. Missing this maintenance puts in danger everyone nearby. It may coast for a while, but inevitably your car will be destroyed for lack of maintenance.

Your marriage is no different. It needs regular attention. Understanding your husband, his needs, and his joys is vital to knowing how to give him the attention that will provide exponential rewards for your marriage. Guard your time with your husband. Protect the marriage bed. Do not let others' demands (kids and otherwise) overrule your priorities. This is your responsibility as a wife. It is vital to invest in your marriage. If your time, money, and life choices don't reflect your priorities, it is time to get your life in line with what truly is *most* important to you.

Notes From Ms. Susan:

Since the beginning, we always agreed our marriage would be our first priority over parenting. So even as we talked about having children we always agreed that our relationship trumped anything else that happened.

Write in your Workbook #31. Reread your goal for your marriage (update it if other aspects have been revealed) and decide on specific actions that you need to A) stop doing and B) start doing. Write what to do to get your life in proper balance with your life's priorities. Getting clear on what changes you need to make is the first step in moving towards them. Be very specific.

Prioritize Lovemaking

How often should you have sex with your husband? You are more aware of your needs and your husband's needs than I am. You should get that answer from him. As a general rule, I would encourage 2-5 times per week. I know our marriage is the strongest and most fulfilling for both of us, if we make love about every other day. If this seems crazy to you, I'm glad you're reading this book! The most important person in your life is worth quite a bit more than 1 hour of your time and effort every other day. Don't you spend at least 1 hour every other day with a friend on the phone, over coffee, or across the cubicle? It is not too much to dedicate this to the most important human relationship in your life. If the first lady were knocking on your door and wanted an hour of your time, every other day you'd happily give it. Yet, the president's wife will not give you years of joy, pay your bills, love your heart--yet you'd deem her more important than your own husband? Your husband is worth it. *Lovemaking must be a regular part of your life.* It needs to be a priority in your life. If it seems like a lot right now, trust me, in a couple of weeks you'll be thanking me. In a couple of years, you will be looking back with happy tears streaming down your face at your amazing marriage.

I am writing this while at a coffee shop down the street from my house. All this talk of priorities is getting me encouraged to wake my phenomenal husband up with some pleasure. Would you excuse me? While I'm gone, write in your Workbook #32. Take time to decide how many times per week you will commit to making love to your husband. Now take out your calendar and figure out exactly when you can have these love encounters.

Schedule It

It may seem completely unsexy, but scheduling sex may be the best way to make sure it happens. You may think it takes out all the fun and spontaneity. I assure you a healthy diet of scheduled sex makes the spontaneous encounters much more easy and enjoyable. Lacking the first, you may never get to the latter or it will be far too few and far in between.

Before you were married, I bet you scheduled your dates. You didn't just assume both of you would be at the same place at the same time, did you? Well, thankfully, now the place is taken care of, but you both may not necessarily be on the *same page* of mental and physical readiness at the same time. Either you can schedule these love encounters on your own calendar (and it may seem more spontaneous to him) or you can share the plan with your hubby in a fun and sexy way. Imagine having a Friday evening planned 'engagement' where you hint at it throughout the day or two leading up. Dropping a note in his work bag: "I can't wait to be in your arms tonight," or sending some steamy text messages while anticipating the evening's events. I am sure this will only increase the excitement of the evening and when you fall into each other's embrace. The seemingly mundane scheduling turns into a home run for your sex life. Also, any anxiety or pressure of initiation and risk of rejection is alleviated because it was planned together. Give this a try, there is only good to come from it.

Whether Or Not You're In The Mood

As you know, we women are wired differently than men. This is not news. We do not get turned on nearly as easily or as frequently as men. I mentioned, generally speaking, women have to commit in their mind to make love before we 'feel' anything. Here's a secret, woman to woman: acting like you're turned on will actually turn you on. I'm not kidding. I cannot remember a time it hasn't worked for me. It requires some effort in the beginning, but does produce great rewards. I do *not* mean faking it. Setting your attitude to "sexy" is the first step to getting yourself in the mood. For men it generally happens more spontaneously and less intentionally. Now, add kids, bills, arguments, schedules, and every life-concern into the mix and if you don't carefully plan your lovemaking it gets pushed to the wayside and might happen once a month, if that. Which is by no means appropriate lovemaking maintenance.

Why is scheduling love making helpful? I am a planner and I need a jumpstart to get my mind focused and ready to really enjoy the process. If I'm really good, I'll make sure I've had a shower, shaved, lotioned up, brushed my teeth, and put on my favorite perfume. All the while doing Sexy Self-Talk. I'll talk more about this. That's right, I take time to get my mind in the game and you should, too. Literally put it on my calendar. I don't always stick to the time exactly, but it helps me to remember and keep it on my mind for the day. I encourage you to plan your love-making. Sex is a huge aspect of marital bliss for you and your honey. It should *not* be an afterthought.

Notes from Ms. Susan:

We have had many, many years of great passion in our intimacy. Three maybe four times a week, probably. Peni as well. I mean, everything was really good. Then we had some really exhausting years. For us, babies and children was a brief season. Yes, you have a couple of years with each child where it is challenging.

But then there were times when we're running kids around, doing all the busy things Americans do (probably a whole other conversation). But just keeping our kids very busy and in all the interests and activities that they had, and just falling into bed dead tired at 10 or 11 at night. And, you know, that wasn't so great.

We have always made an effort to maintain a sex life. I know couples who will go like a month without having sex. We always really---well, maybe we didn't always hit every week--but we always tried to hit every week. Hopefully even a little more than that.

Prepare and Be Sexy

Many men could have spent the day working the fields, gotten humiliated in front of coworkers, come home sweaty, dirty, and starving. But he'd gladly put all that on hold to have a quickie just after walking in the door. In fact that'd probably make his horrible day somewhat decent. Speaking for myself, I am nowhere near that. If I'm not careful, socks on the floor can be enough to get me distracted and throw off my mood. The thing is, I know that about myself. It is natural for women to be easily distracted than men when it comes to lovemaking. You're not alone. But we need to acknowledge this and problem-solve accordingly. Let's think about you. Consider the events, distractors or stressors that take you completely out of the mood. Think through what makes you uncomfortable having sex. Some ideas to get you going: feeling full from food, feeling unclean, missing normal make up, doubting physical beauty, unshaven areas, messy house, thinking about extended-family drama, thinking about my to-do lists...

Write in your Workbook #33. What are your distractors? What thoughts come to mind and throw off your focus? Once you get clear on the items that throw you off, you can plan around them to get you to success.

Pleasure Preparation

When you have an *important* appointment on your calendar, I make sure to prepare for it, right? For example, a job interview. You get clean and fresh, wear the appropriate outfit, block out negative thoughts, condition your mind with positive self-talk, review and print your resume. You'll probably re-review your value and credentials to build your confidence. You also think about your prospective employer and what they will be looking for in a candidate. Your important love encounter appointment can follow a similar path to ensure success.

In my case, I like to have the house relatively picked up (not perfect, but I don't want to be running through my "should-haves" while in the act). I like to make sure the kids are sleeping (so I don't have to concern myself with interruptions). I also really feel sexier with freshly shaven legs, so I have a habit to do that during every shower. I also feel sexier with shaven lady areas. (A quick tip: if you have a problem with razor burn in these sensitive areas, use a men's battery-powered electric razor. It works well on dry hair and skin, just be careful to not nick yourself. Then take a shower afterwards to get all the trimmings washed away. It's not as close of a shave, but it isn't painful and still gives you that shaven confidence). Of course, you should prepare according to what your hubby prefers. If you do not know, ask him. He probably has a preference and it would make you feel more confident by meeting that desire. I also like to feel fresh, so I make sure I take a quick shower or in a pinch use a washcloth for quick freshness. Smelling nice helps me to feel sexy, so I spritz some of my favorite perfume. I plan out what outfit and lingerie I will wear.

Write in your Workbook #34. Looking at your previous distractor list, what are ways that you should prepare for sex? Knowing your and your hubby's preferences, what preparation will make you feel ready to enjoy?

Sexy Self-Talk

I mentioned engaging in positive self-talk. If positive self-talk is unusual for you, start getting used to it by speaking it aloud. Eventually you'll get used to doing this and it and it will be more automatic in your head. I have the Sexy Self-Talk Outline included in your course materials. Post this list in the bathroom or in a more private place where only you can pull it out and read it. Use your name and speak aloud each item. Explain to yourself how much you enjoy making love to your husband. As you start practicing Sexy Self-Talk, the amounts of items to be grateful for will grow. Be *very* positive. You need to develop a winning mindset for lovemaking.

The winning mindset starts by *willing yourself* to be positive. Get the picture of a wonderful sexual encounter in your mind before you even see your hubby. Regardless of your previous mindset, you can change your thoughts by speaking the right ones out loud. Start speaking them before you feel them. That's how faith works right? In faith, you have to start speaking how you want to be feeling. If you want to be more turned on by your husband, start telling yourself how hot he makes you. Also, start focusing on the areas of your sex life that are wonderful. Describe how much you appreciate his desire for you. Change your mind by changing your words. Don't play the victim any longer. Don't pretend things will change once your feelings change--that is just stagnating. Remember this is the most important relationship in your life. If you'd go through this kind of preparation to ensure a positive interview, how much more should you work on making positive intimate experiences with your husband. He is more important than a boss.

Be proactive. If you want things to change, you have to start changing them. This may feel like work at first. Anything new is uncomfortable at first. But as you do, and do, *and do*, it will become comfortable and fun. Soon, it will even feel natural and your new positive mindset will have replaced the old. You will look back, just weeks from now, and realize your sexual mindset has completely shifted for the better.

Write in your Workbook #35. Write out a script for yourself to prepare your mind for sex. Follow the outline in your course materials. Practice this script now. And get in the habit of practicing your Sexy Self-Talk to get your mind ready for enjoying.

Steamy To Do:

Practice your Sexy Self-Talk before initiating intimacy with your hubby tonight. Notice how confident and desirous you feel. And then enjoy!

SECTION IV

Love Your

Husband

Are You Unintentionally Hurting Him?

Your Insecurities Pain Him

Are you the kind of lady who likes roses on Valentine's days? Do you enjoy a special date planned for your anniversary? Or do you expect a surprise gift from your hubby on your birthday? These may seem like no-brainers for you. But for him, it can be very scary. It feels like his abilities as a husband are on trial. I misunderstood my husband in this area for a long time. I thought that D didn't want to bring me flowers or celebrate special days with me. But in the back of my mind, I would make up a story that he didn't think I was worth these niceties. These are important to me, so it hurt when he missed an occasion or put no thought into a celebration-worthy day.

We eventually were able to uncover the truth. He felt vulnerable every time these occasions came around. He was so worried about whether I would like what he prepared, so often he would choose the safer route of doing our 'normal' routines instead of anything special. Of course these routines I am typically satisfied with, but on these days they would make me disappointed. What D couldn't understand was the pain he caused me. His "forgetting" was avoiding the risk of being judged or letting me down. Plus he unconsciously thought that ignoring them would make my expectation go away. Instead it caused significant pain for me. He didn't understand the pain his insecurities were causing me.

We are similar. As a woman, I failed to realize the pain I was causing my husband by withholding my body from him. Whenever I gain a few pounds or maybe had a bad-eating day, it is hard for me to indulge in a sexual experience because of my own insecurities. I was self-conscious about my body and thought it wasn't a big deal if I didn't engage intimately with him a couple of times. I failed to realize the pain he went through by my disinterest in sex. For me, I thought he couldn't possibly be attracted to someone who had gained those extra pounds.

That is the issue. We think our body is just about us and our choices around sex are just about our feelings. However, your husband longs to see and be with you intimately. It does cause him pain if you cannot bring yourself to engage sensually. Just like my husband was causing me pain due to his own nervousness. It was not intentional selfishness that was stopping him. He was concerned that I would judge him. Your self-consciousness is most likely causing your honey pain. At the least, it is robbing him of a more fantastic and fulfilling love life.

Self-Consciousness Isn't Reality

Movies have messed up our understanding of what it feels like to be sexy. It seems like only women with perfect bodies and faces can be confident in bed. That could not be farther from the truth. God made you with a unique sexual appeal that no one possesses but you. Everyone feels vulnerable taking off their clothes. The only reason actresses in the movies don't seem self-conscious is because they are professional *actors*. It's their *job* to make it look effortless. Even the skinniest, most proportionate women feel nervous about their bodies. The hottest women on magazine covers today will age just like the rest of us. Eventually, they too, will have worries about the state of their appearance. If they are putting their trust in their looks now, their feelings of body-confidence will melt into self-doubt. Everyone feels nervous at times. Most of us feel inadequate in a saucy teddy. That doesn't mean your husband doesn't enjoy it, even while you feel nervous. If you could see through his eyes, I bet you'd agree you look great too.

Have you ever felt you looked terrible at an event? Then weeks later, a couple of pictures from the party revealed a darn good-looking lady. Our feelings about how we look are not to be trusted. Self-consciousness is a robber. It vandalizes all that we hold dear. If we start feeling self-conscious and our husband gazes off into the distance, we can come up with a story in our heads that he is disinterested or, worse, daydreaming about someone else. Both are probably ludacris. I have wreaked havoc on my marriage during a time when I felt particularly uncomfortable in my own skin. I thought he had a wandering eye when we were out walking together. It was a beautiful summer day and we were really enjoying each other's company. I tried to shake the concern, but eventually I asked him. He was surprised and immediately felt attacked. A storm cloud seemed to roll out over our previously delightful afternoon. He felt like all the good he was doing in our relationship (which was plenty) was totally irrelevant and that he could do nothing right in my eyes. Eventually the upset subsided and he clarified that he in fact had not been checking out the woman in booty shorts. Then it hit me: my own insecurity caused me to make this up in my mind. Then, his defensive response made me feel even more discomfort and insecurity. This was a trap laid by the enemy. Both of us felt pain. Here we were enjoying a wonderful time together and the enemy wants to steal that. He wants us to turn against each other and insecurity is a very effective tool.

Fearing Man Is A Trap

Instead, we ladies have to be resolved in God's opinion of us and not waver when we fear our own husband's opinions. First of all, our insecurities may be completely unfounded. Secondly, our husband is not God and he is not perfect. He may make mistakes, have unrealistic expectations, or just forget to reassure and compliment us. The Bible explains that we should not gain or wane in confidence based upon someone else's opinions of us. The Bible calls this "fear of man". We should only fear God. "Fear of man will prove to be a snare, but whoever trusts in the Lord is kept safe" (Prov 29:25). Being concerned with the judgments of our husbands seems like a fine thing. Shouldn't we be interested in what he thinks of us? In some ways, yes. But if we are living for his approval, that is very unsteady ground. It keeps us in bondage to what he thinks, wants, or even what we *think* he wants. Instead of being a confident woman in our own right, we are ensnared in our perception of his judgments.

Recently, I was reading a post about reasons women do not engage in sex. The comments following from husbands gripped me. So many men had the same sad story. They explained that they loved their wives. They helped around the house, supported the family, gave great care to their kids. But their wives were completely uninterested in sex and generally refused. The pain in these men's messages reveal sex as a central part of their hearts and lives. I imagine many of these wives are not mad or bitter at their husbands (as the husbands think). I bet these wives are scared and looking for reasons to be mad, so they can avoid the insecurity they feel in the marriage bed. However, wives need to push through and value their sex life over their own comfort.

Do not let your mind wander down the road of self-consciousness, it is a trap. God's truth is clear. We are fearfully and wonderfully made. We are the apple of God's eye, the object of His desire and delight. We are more than enough for our husbands. God made us uniquely beautiful and sexually appealing to our husbands. God has big work for us to do and focusing on how our bodies compared to a societal standard undermines all that He wants to do in and through us. Jesus rebukes Peter for being concerned with worldly concerns over the concerns of the Father. He very strongly says, "you do not have in mind the concerns of God, but merely human concerns" (Matt 16:23). When considering the priorities of God, our silly insecurities pale and seem completely ridiculous. Let us take a stand against self-conscious thinking and have in mind the concerns of God.

God gives a plan for victory with the devil's mind games. "Submit yourselves, then, to God. Resist the devil, and he will flee from you" (James 4:7). Submit means to put yourself under the leadership of another. Do let your mind be subject to God's word, His ways and Himself. Invite Him into your head when these thoughts attack. Tell God what you're thinking about. Ask God to show you truth. Your thoughts are fruits of what is going on in your heart. He is the one who can make your inner parts good. Ask Him to change your heart and be diligent to submit to Him. "Resist the devil" by *not* succumbing to the temptation. Place your mind on something other than the self-conscious thoughts. When you are resolved not to yield to the enemy's attack, you will gain victory in this area. I believe the enemy will see he cannot get a foothold in your mind in this area and will stop attacking it.

Write in your Workbook #36. Take the time to write how the enemy has attacked your mind with self-consciousness. Try to think of the scenarios and instances when it is most difficult to resist his lies. Share these with a trusted friend. Ask her to pray for you and will agree to check in on you and how you're submitting to God and resisting the devil in this area.

Steamy To Do:

Wearing something a little skimpy, sit next to your husband on the couch. Begin massaging his back. Tell him how much you love and value him. Start a conversation about how sexy you find his body, touch and show him exactly what you love about it.

Understanding His Desire

What Men and Women Want from Marriage

The love a woman wants from a marriage and the love a man wants are the same. However, the action of love manifests very differently in each gender. Women, generally, desire to feel understood, cherished, and secure. These desires are so central that women often feel men *should* provide a listening ear, give us regular compliments, and have a steady job to support us. We feel so strongly about these because they are *our* emotional needs. We understand them. We need them. They are necessary at our core. We feel pain when our husband denies us those things. Your man desires these as well, to a degree. To a far greater degree, he desires to feel respected, capable, and honored in your marriage. These are core needs for your man. He feels hurt, alone, and disappointed without these vital pieces in his marriage. These items are generally significantly affected by your interaction in the bedroom. He desires his advances are embraced and reciprocated. When you honor, respect, and make him feel capable in the bedroom, his emotional needs are met. Sex is *very* important to your husband.

Sex Is Vital To His Heart

There was a time in my marriage, due to health issues, that we weren't able to make love. I remember gently asking my husband how he was feeling about it. He said it wasn't a problem because he understood the reason. When I inquired more about his feelings, he tenderly shared, "I just don't feel like I can love you as deeply without making love to you". We hear men say things innocently like this and it gives us a glimpse into their souls. His desire for sex should be considered a way of meeting his emotional need for love. A need just as valid as our need to share and be treasured in the depths of our hearts. Sex is a vital way your husband loves you and feels loved by you. A male friend confided in me the pain he felt about his wife's rejection. It hurt him to have his wife nearby, but she would not engage with him physically. It was the same pain I hear (and have felt) from women friends who are starved for their husband's affection. Sex for your husband is a vital desire and necessary for his fulfillment in marriage.

His desire for sex is strong. As we are well aware, some men have this desire met unhealthily by sexually taking advantage or not respecting women's choices. In response, many in our society paint a picture of men's sexuality as that of a sex-crazed animal who doesn't care for the person with whom he is lying. Society expects men to have an unquenchable, unrestrained sexual appetite. You probably are familiar with the "double standard". Phrases like the following are commonly heard. "If she didn't want it, she shouldn't have worn that outfit", "Of course he slept with her--he's a man" or "He just wants one thing from her and that's it". It is true that there are men who could care less for who they are with as long as this sexual need is met. But, this is a distortion of the beauty God created in the sexual desire within men.

Within marriage, men's sexual passion can be a powerful force for good in your union. Yes, he is still a man. These sexual desires are strong in him, just as they are in every other man. But, it is vital you understand your husband's desire for sex is a holy, God-given desire. Sex binds two people together like *nothing* else can. It literally changes chemicals in the body and redirects brain synapses. Men's desire for sex is a motivating factor for it to happen again and again. A wife should not shame her husband for expressing himself sexually and his desire for her. An expert, Dr. Kerner, says "For men, the sex act is the primary conduit for expressing their feelings." In other words, while women generally deem closeness a prerequisite for engaging in sex, for a man, having sex is probably the best, sometimes only, path to achieving a true sense of intimacy with a romantic partner" [1].

The way you desire to show love to him is different than the way he desires to show love to you. I like to love my husband by having a deep discussion walking arm-in-arm while walking in the park then cuddling on the couch at home. His way of loving me is making passionate, orgasmic, intimate love. Though we both enjoy each of these, our go-to form of giving and receiving love generally differs in this way. God made us with these differences to ensure that we learn to serve one another. With these differences, we become mutually selfless in our marriages and experience the fullness of intimacy. God wants us to focus on the needs of others. That is why we were initially so attracted to the differences we see in our mate. Your man wants sex. It's not because he wants to dominate, use, or control you. Sex is just his principle way of loving you and feeling loved by you.

Gentle With His Desire

It is likely that your husband has experienced pain in regards to his sexuality. You may not know the story of his first erection or wet dream. I'll give you the punchline: it was embarrassing. In those early years, he may have been humiliated by friends at school. He may have felt embarrassed from his mother when she happened upon him exploring. He may have dealt with deep shame in sexual addictions as a young man. There are many pains in the heart of your husband that you may not know. I encourage you to be gentle with him. You are his confidante. You are the one person who, slowly, he'll open up to as he feels safe. When he can share his burdens with you and lets down his guard, there is a healing comfort to this. You need to be receptive and gentle. As a wife, at times you'll need to look past your own issues and realize he may be hurting and numb to some things because of his past. He may feel ashamed of his own desires or insecurities.

What if you take the first step? What if you accept that your husband needs connection through sex to fulfill deep needs? Could you move past the hurt and discomfort you may feel to serve him in the way he best receives love? My theory is: no matter who started it or whose fault it is, it can change if *you* take the first step in love and gentleness. It's not really my theory, it's modeled by Jesus. If you wait for your husband to make the first move, you could be waiting a very long time and waste many years or perhaps your whole marriage. There's no need to be "right". Just work to *move the ball forward*. Get your marriage on the right path regardless of the means or humility it requires.

What a Man Wants

Your husband wants you to find him sexy. He wants you to appreciate his hard work, professionally and around the house. He wants you to love to be with him in intimacy. Amidst the joys and stressors of life, he wants his wife to want him and sexually desire him. His dream is for regular lovemaking. You should ask him. He might admit to wishing it would happen multiple times every day. He wants a wife who is confident in her body and will initiate sex because she enjoys the way he makes her feel. He gets so much pleasure watching you enjoy making love to him.

He gets nervous too: that you might not be enjoying yourself, that you don't find him attractive, that his body isn't good enough, and that he's not doing a good enough job in bed. He wants to love you this way. He wants to rock your world in bed. It turns him on to see you turned on. He feels more like a man when he can make you orgasm. He would love to hear you go wild because of his touch. When you initiate sex, you are telling him that you desire him. You are telling him that you want him. You are telling him that he can and does satisfy your sexual needs. He wants a woman who seduces him. He wants his wife to give him a lap dance and a strip tease. To be sensual with his member and caress it with a deep love and appreciation. He wants her to feel confident in her lovemaking. I'm wondering what is going through your mind as you read this, dear sister? Does this sound like your husband?

Write in your Workbook #37 about how similar the man described is to your husband. Do you know how he feels in these areas? Have you talked with him about his sexual passion? Are there areas that you can grow as a wife to meet your honey's wants and needs?

The Male Mind

It's not very original of me to say that you and your husband think differently. We as women forget this truth. Or we think our specific husbands are exempt from it. We assume that our husbands are just the same as us, with different body parts. You think he should inherently understand you and your way of thinking. As I've repeated in different ways throughout this course, you need to understand him *first*. Men are wired in a way to be very aware of sex and sexual cues. It is a major force in their psyche. Just take a cursory look at our society. How many scantily clad women do you see on TV, magazine covers, billboards, on the streets, and in advertisements per day? It's shocking how many messages are aimed *first and foremost* for sexual appeal.

These ads are marketing to men. Personally, I am not a huge fan of seeing cleavage and cheeks all over the place. Most women feel the same way. But men are immediately and naturally drawn to these images. Though many men also wish these images weren't all over the place--it takes their attention immediately. Marketers are smart. They know men are attracted to these visuals and will make them pay attention. However, the marketing subliminally is advertising to women too. They are telling us, "Look, this is what men want and this is what you're not. So, buy this diet pill, purchase that skin cream, wear this swimsuit, and add this to your wardrobe! Otherwise your man might go after this woman..." Consider for a minute the styles of women's clothes. They are tight and revealing because they appeal to men. Women are not as sexually aroused by visuals, thus men's styles are much more modest. It is common to see a woman in tight yoga pants and men find that very appealing. But many women might involuntarily dry-heave if we saw a man in tight yoga pants.

Of course, our society has taken the act of sex out of the environment God designed. The imagery plastered all over is supposed to be intimate excitement enjoyed in the bedroom between husband and wife. That is what should happen. But it is not what is happening. Your husband is a Christian, but that does not mean he is devoid of sexual desire and impulses. He is one of "those men" who is attracted to all this sexual imagery. God made him and every man with these inclinations. As wise wives, we need to understand how our man thinks. When your husband sees female curves, they are naturally interesting to him. In pursuit of holiness, he should turn his eyes away and guard his thoughts that he might not lust after another woman and sin.

I do not want you to be unhealthily preoccupied with these

temptations. However, you must be aware that that is a temptation he deals with every day--many, many times. As his wife, you are his only holy source of sexual pleasure, visually and physically. Again, God made it this way. We must recognize that God's design is to provide a context for your husband's sexuality to be fulfilled and thrive in your marriage. God designed this part of your husband so that your passion could burn brightly in marriage. He could uphold you and you could uphold him, tightly bound to one another.

Helping Your Honey Into Holiness

You have the privilege and pleasure to play that role in his life. You have the privilege of meeting his sexual needs. This is good news. God was wise enough to endow men with this great need, so that they would learn kindness, gentleness, and selflessness -- all vital to making their wife happy. He would learn how to have patience, how to listen and how to have strength in God. A happy wife is much more likely to enjoy and have frequent sex. As your husband seeks to become more like Jesus, you can play a vital role in helping him keep his eyes and mind pure. I do *not* mean: you can cure your husband's wandering eyes, unfaithfulness, or other sinful sexual addictions. If there is sin that he is struggling with, you are not responsible for that. However, you can provide life-saving support to your husband who may be drowning in these struggles.

I'll give you an example that hopefully will illustrate my point. When my husband and I started dating, I was struggling with a serious eating disorder. This developed into a sickness which started in my mind. In isolation, I would allow myself to go into self-pity and a kind of depression. I had been very hurt by my past and bulimia was a way to get out of those horrible feelings. At that time, I would engage in this practice about once a day. I was maintaining loose professional and personal friendships and no one knew anything about this. I started to feel safe in our relationship and I began to trust D's deep care for me and my heart. I could sense that he wanted me to be fully alive, free, and happy. Eventually, I shared it with him. He was concerned. He wanted me to feel loved and treasured and not so consumed with my figure and other stressors that it led me to this sin. He never let on that this hurt him personally. As you could imagine, he would have been hurt realizing he "wasn't enough" to make his girlfriend happy and healthy. As I opened up to him, I felt his deep compassion towards me. I started to feel more powerful and able to resist. I felt less enslaved by this secret. Every time it happened I felt D and my relationship was a safe place for me to share. He kindly listened, held me in my tears and shame, and loved me back on track. He was trustworthy and did not share this with anyone. By God's grace, I began to feel emboldened to share and gain support from family and friends as well. These people knowing this issue was truly the push I needed to stand against the temptation. By God's grace, I was able to stop the habit completely. Did D cause my sin? No. But he was able to love me, not take it personally, not judge me, and lend strength and support to help me get out of it.

Responding To Sexual Addiction

That is the potential I see for wives supporting their husbands out of sexual sin. You are a significant part of his life. You can provide life-giving support to him in his time of need. Sexual addictions such as pornography form for many reasons. Many are rooted in past curiosity, abuse, or even inappropriate role models who encouraged the behavior. Addicts need a lot of support, love, and honesty to get free. You can be a major factor in helping him get free and stay free. Your husband's sexual sin feels like it is against you. It is painful. You will need to work through this pain and with support move towards forgiveness. The truth is he is first and foremost rejecting God.

He is feeling a lot of shame and guilt because of this force in his life. He knows it is wrong. He knows he should not engage in this. The more you learn about this addiction, the more you will be able to move to a place of forgiveness and problem-solving. Porn provides a chemical release in the brain that is addictive in nature. If your husband has struggled with this for years, it has developed into a habit providing an instant orgasmic release. It has become a physiological habit. Some men are more strongly tempted to pursue this kind of release if they feel inadequate in their marriage bed. They may feel they have to perform (this may have roots in the past even if it is not be a current reality). This mindset may cause a lot of anxiety for him which is not present in the pornography experience.

I encourage you to find support. You need support to heal and to help your husband get free. In the midst of your feelings, try to remember you are the protector of his reputation and his heart. Share this struggle only with trustworthy friends and Christian leaders who can hold your marriage in prayer and support you through the pain. This is a *very* common struggle but it is still a topic widely misunderstood.

It is not easy to get free from pornography addiction. But God can save your husband from this struggle. God can even erase the memories. It is not easy at all for you as the wife. It preys on your insecurities and makes you feel inadequate. Jesus wants your marriage to be solid. He wants you two to finish the race together. As hard as it may seem, if you can be honest with the hurt but also forgive him, you will be moving forward on the right track. God forgives you for far greater sins. Ask God for strength and guidance on how to forgive and how to move forward.

How His Drive Works

As a sensual wife, you may be a powerful force in protecting his mind from wandering into tempting territory. You may know, when a man goes without sex for long enough, there is a physical and natural response to deal with this need. He will ejaculate in his sleep often accompanied with a sexual dream. The testes are working to fill again with millions of semen all of the time. God made your husband to have regular sexual experiences. You have the ability and the power to give him regular intimacy which helps him stay pure and focused in his thoughts and happy in his heart.

It may help to consider how you feel after a really affectionate date. When you and your husband have lots of deep conversations and he gives you sincere compliments. I know if I go without affection from my husband for a while I begin to doubt my husband's love for me. My mind starts unrealistically wandering to think of my friends' hubbies in comparison. Or I begin to get jealous of the openly affectionate couple on the train. Imagine that your husband and every man had a sex tank that's constantly filling with fuel. When the tank gets to a certain level, your husband's control of his thoughts and temptations wanes. But once he makes love to you, the tank goes back down to zero and there is some time until the fuel fills to that fuel level again. You have the opportunity to keep his tank regularly "serviced".

Of course it is possible for men to go without. I believe God has given men a grace to be single. Without use, their sexual desires lessen. However, in marriage, we are not to "deprive each other" (1 Cor 7:5). The fire of passion should be ablaze to give you both the bonding necessary for oneness and an effectual marriage. You want to fill his needs and desires. Aim at open communication around this subject so you both can understand each other's needs and desires more deeply. I would also encourage you to be very curious about his sexual drive and needs. Try not to cast judgment on his desires. They are God's gift, and it is important for you two to understand each other fully in this area.

Write in your Workbook #38. Have you ever considered the struggle your husband goes through every day to keep his mind pure? Remember his struggles and consider how you can support him and his purity.

What To Do With His Drive

Many women misunderstand their husbands' sex drive. They see it as something he should be able to control and turn off when inappropriate. Women think at times it even gets annoying. Of course he can control his actions. But the drive is natural. What I think these women miss is how wonderful his drive really is. It is a *really* good thing. Without it, for many marriages, sex would be a thing for only newlyweds. God designed sex to be something enjoyed regularly throughout every season of life in marriage. Some seasons of life are more difficult than others and the bonding that lovemaking increases makes those times easier. Couples who have gone through significant tragedy and stayed together have said that making love provides a unity and connection that was vital in those seasons. You both can connect, enjoy, and experience a physical release even when words would not be helpful. God has many divine purposes for the love act. The world was not populated without this vital piece of God's plan. It is central to his first commandment to humans. We wives need to remember the blessing of a strong libido. Experts say that your frequency and satisfaction of sex can be a dipstick for a marriage [2]. Not having or maintaining regular lovemaking in your marriage is an indicator of trouble. (If this doesn't describe your husband's drive and his is much lower, there is hope. In the Troubleshooting section I included some helpful solutions.)

Love Breathes Freedom

If you feel compelled to make love every time he wants it, you will not enjoy it. It may become a barrier or a source of resentment for you. I do not want to encourage you to make love out of compulsion. I want to give you the understanding of how significant sex is to your husband. More than likely, it is *far* more significant than it is to you. If you have an understanding of his unique desire, you can aim to meet that. It won't always be possible. There will be times you will need to say "I love you. But tonight, I'm just too tired honey". Love can only exist in freedom. That is why God gave us free will, so when we turn to Him in love it is true and real. Love breathes freedom. You seek to please and love your husband on your own free will, not out of compulsion. Check your heart, make sure you're making love for the right reasons. Resentment undermines love. If resentment has crept into your heart, realize it is your responsibility to forgive and move forward in honesty.

Notes From Ms. Susan:

Sex can be a sacrifice for a woman. It really can. Many times you don't feel like it. But he needs that. He really does. I talk to some women and they're just like "yuck". But sex is important. It really is important. And I think that is a part of understanding your husband. If my husband has been turned down by me a couple of times consecutively, he just won't really ask. And that doesn't mean that he doesn't want it. It just means he doesn't want to infringe on my space. I realize that I need to initiate too. Particularly if I have turned him down a couple of times.

Find Your Ideal

Some women don't realize their frequency or method of rejection of their husband's sexual advances actually wound him. You should not feel compelled to make love every time your husband is in the mood (every time he has an erection is probably physically impossible to satisfy anyway). It helps me to have an ideal in my head and trying to be pretty close to that. As I mentioned, our ideal as a couple is to make love every other day, give or take. I also try to bring it up every couple of weeks when we're both in a good emotional space. I want to know how he's feeling about our sex life. I like to ask him if he feels like we're in a good spot. D is not a natural sharer, so I try to ask open-ended questions that help him to express his feelings in a safe and positive space, ie: "How are you feeling about our love making?" "Are there things I can do to make it better for you?" "How do you think we can make it more satisfying for both of us?" etc. Because this is a habit at this point, he'll generally ask the same questions to me. This gives me a chance to share anything in my heart as well.

Notes from Ms. Susan:

I think it is very important that you understand your own husbands' sex drive. Because it is just as individual as ours are. Make every effort to meet that to some degree. You need to really make an effort to make sure his needs at the most basic level are met. Because the reality of it is if they're not met by you, they may end up being met by fantasy or other things. And that's not a place you want to go.

Start a Sex life Check In Habit

I would encourage you to discuss your husband's desires with him. Make it a habit in your marriage to do a Sex life Check In. Every couple of weeks, check in with him about how he is feeling about your sex life. In these honest conversations, you should be very open and curious and not take offense. Encourage him to be honest. You *want* him to be open and if you cast judgement or get defensive it won't happen in the future. As this becomes a regular topic, there is less pressure or awkwardness when you really need to talk about something. Making this a common occurrence provides a safe space to discuss how you're feeling. Remember the challenge of vulnerability is surmounted when you do the hard work of being vulnerable first.

Steamy To Do:

While your hubby is in a good emotional space and he's sitting, straddle him and begin kissing his neck. Ask him, "Baby if you could take me at any time, whenever you wanted me, how often would you want to make love?"

Communication is Central

Language About The Bedroom

There is a common but unacceptable disconnect in marriage. The lack of communication in marriages surrounding sex is not ok. I find this very sad. We women need to process, usually out loud. We need to hear that things are going well in this vital area. We need to talk about what is not going ok. We need to know that our husband is enjoying our sexual experiences together. We need to know he cares that we are also enjoying it. If these conversations aren't happening regularly, a change needs to take place.

Notes From Ms. Susan:

Ms. Susan, you've seen so many marriages starting and ending and every place in between. Have you found that a significant element to marriages breaking is the sexual piece?

I don't know if that is a cause or an effect. I would say that it is always an important missing link towards the end or in marriages in crisis. But I don't know if that is what caused it. Or that it is that way because of all the other things. I do think that communication is the most important. I absolutely believe people can have happy and strong marriages without sex, if they have to. Because we know sometimes they do. But, I don't think that anybody can have a very strong marriage without communication.

How to Talk to Him... About *This*

How do you tell your husband that you're going to turn things up a few dozen notches in the bedroom department? You know your husband best, so you'll be able to tweak these suggestions in a way that is best for him. I always find openness is the best policy. You want him to be helping you on this journey. As you practice and progress in feeling comfortable and confident as a sexual woman, he will definitely take notice whether you tell him or not. Why should you have an honest conversation beforehand with your hubby? Because he is in this with you.

What we will discuss in the next section is all about his body. His body and his preferences only he can truly know. You want him to be on the same page to encourage and help you. You want to avoid uncomfortable and potentially hurtful moments for you, if he misunderstands your intentions. You need a very encouraging environment to take new risks in this area. So, he needs to know your plans. A simple, upfront conversation can alleviate concerns. Realize that he wants you to come into your own as a confident and free woman in the bedroom. He'll likely be so excited for your courage in approaching the topic (something he's probably thanking God for!). Honest conversations are key to a lasting, loving connection your marriage, in the bedroom and outside of it.

Honesty With Wisdom

I'd like to talk about honesty a little. This is the context in which I will encourage honest communication. Sometimes people are brash or even hurtful in the name of being "honest". I encourage you to be completely honest with your husband. However, I would caution you to remember that your honesty should be tempered with wisdom. We want to be wise in how we speak to our husbands. "Wisdom from above is first of all pure, peace-loving, gentle, willing to yield, full of mercy and good fruits--without hypocrisy and without partiality" (James 3:17).

If that isn't enough to convince you, that you need to pray and seek wisdom when approaching your mate, let's look at Jesus' example. Jesus always used wisdom when speaking to people. He was very careful to consider *who* he was talking to. He met people where they were at that time in their lives. He challenged them, but he was not a one-size-fits-all kind of man. He spoke truth, but he used wisdom and compassion. After saving her life, Jesus told the woman caught in the act of adultery, "'Then neither do I condemn you,' Jesus declared. 'Go now and leave your life of sin'" (John 8:11). He seemed quite forgiving and kind to her. But he told the rich young ruler who had followed *every* law from his youth, "If you want to be perfect, go, sell your possessions and give to the poor, and you will have treasure in heaven. Then come, follow me." (Matt 19:21). It seems like Jesus was easy on the "sinful" woman and demanded everything from the already "righteous" young man.

It was wisdom. Jesus saw what the rich young ruler was mature in his relationship with God and could handle more significant instruction. The man came to Jesus seeking for more understanding to have a deeper walk with God. Jesus directed him in that way. He showed him the next thing that was separating him from God. But the adulterous woman, who was nowhere near that level of maturity, needed to understand the first step: Jesus is merciful and willing to forgive her. That truth, tempered by wisdom, gave her the confidence and understanding to begin her walk with Him. Maybe a couple of years down the road, she got to a place where Jesus would have asked her to put her treasure in heaven instead of trusting in her bank account also.

Being honest with your husband never means being rude. Truth should always be subject to tact and gentleness, considering to *whom* you speak. Consider your husband. Consider his insecurities, his past, and his heart when bringing up a topic. Pray about talking with your husband. Meditate on the scripture I mentioned: "The wisdom from above is first pure, peace loving, gentle, willing to yield, full of mercy and good fruits [love joy peace, patience, goodness, kindness, faithfulness, gentleness and self-control]--without hypocrisy and without partiality" (James 3:17) Pray with me: *Lord, I ask that you would help me to honor and respect my husband. Help me to speak to him with wisdom. Father, I also ask for confidence to speak to him about this intimate topic. Would you make our marriage into an open and honest place to love and be loved in intimacy? Thank you for your help in this. Amen.*

Fight The Right Fight

Growing up I had some close friends and was privy to a lot of what happened in their home. Their parents' marriages were really challenging and it seemed everything was fair-game during a fight. I mean *everything*. When the mom and dad were mad at each other the rhetorical knives came out with a vengeance. Things from long ago, probably before my friend was born, were screamed across the room (echoing throughout the house). Anything that would hurt the other person was a useful weapon during "battle". The problem is these fights left both sides bleeding with no safe place for refuge. Each side would go to their respective unhealthy coping mechanisms. Witnessing these fights taught me to have strict barriers in my marital arguments. There are certain lines I will not allow myself to cross. I will not allow myself to get angry to the extent that I begin fighting "dirty". This includes bringing up things that I previously forgave and needless insults or criticism. I always try to keep in mind that whatever I say could be carried with D for the rest of our lives. Words cannot be taken back. James says that our words are a fire (James 3:6). A fire can be incredibly helpful--providing warmth, edification, and a life-saving environment within the boundaries of a fireplace. Or it can destroy homes, families, and whole communities if it is left without protective barriers. Our fights follow us into the bedroom whether we realize it or not.

Who Is Your Enemy

A key part to healthy marital communication is to realize that your husband is *not* your enemy. He is the closest one to you and will feel a lot of your pain, but *he* is not the one you're fighting against. "For we wrestle not against flesh and blood but of principalities" (Eph 6:12). It may seem that he is the source of your pain, but remember who the real enemy is. Paul tells us to "be alert and of sober mind. Your enemy the devil prowls around like a roaring lion looking for someone to devour." (1 Pet 5:8). Your marriage and intimacy is hated by the devil. He wants to destroy it all. He knows the power and purpose a healthy marriage possesses. But thank God, you are not fighting against flesh and blood and "for the weapons of our warfare are not of the flesh, but divinely powerful for the destruction of fortresses...and we are taking every thought captive to the obedience of Christ" (2 Cor 10:4-5). So, take time to pray. As you feel the emotions raging and the enemy's tactics starting to wear on you, pause. Ask God fto help you and to show you what is *really* going on and to give you the grace to speak with gentleness and wisdom.

Healthy Fighting Rules

D and I have made some fighting rules together. As you read what we have chosen as a couple, start thinking about what Healthy Fighting Rules would be helpful in your marriage.

1)   Our first boundary is to never walk away from each other during an argument. This is a huge trigger, developed in childhood, for me. If either of us need space, we ask if it's ok to take a break to continue this later. And we do continue it later.

2)   The second thing is to not take the things said in anger or frustration personally. When a harsh phrase is slung, I try to first assume it is because my husband is in the midst of an extreme emotion. Internally, I acknowledge that was hurtful. But, I actively try to get us to a more calm emotional space. After letting the smoke clear a little, I may talk with D about it. I calmly share that the thing he said hurt me. I ask him if there was any truth in it, or was he saying it out of anger. This gives me a more realistic view of what he actually means, instead of addressing it in the heat of the moment and allowing it to explode into much more hurt on both sides.

3)   The third habit we as a couple have developed is to use a number-rating scale. If an issue seems to be very intense for one of us, one of us will ask, "on a scale of 1-10, how serious is this to you?" This is very helpful, because something that feels like a 3 to me, may be an 8 to him. Once I understand how strongly he feels, I can take more care in understanding the root of his strong feeling.

4)   We have adopted a fourth habit I learned from a coworker when working with at risk youth. The students we were working with had abuse in their past. They were hard to handle at times. She told me once, you must "take the fire out of your voice". Generally, when I start to get upset, my voice takes on a shrill and high-pitched quality. The volume of my voice also increases. I have learned this makes D feel like I'm scolding him as though I

were his mother. When speaking this way, he doesn't hear anything but yelling. To him, this tone feels like the utmost disrespect. That is the last way I want him to feel, ever. When I recognize that my voice is becoming fierce, I consciously take a second to "take the fire out" and continue with calm, soft tones that speak respect to my husband.

5) Our fifth and probably most important habit, adopted from Stephen Covey, is "seek first to understand, then to be understood" [3]. My husband and I come from different cultures and languages. This fact makes for many miscommunications. It has also been a blessing because it has taught both of us to be patient. It is so easy especially when emotions are heated to try to make my point heard and *not* hear what D is really saying. We try to understand first and foremost. Only after we fully understand, *then* we try to think about and formulate our own response. This is a discipline that must be practiced at all times.

It is so important to develop some ground rules for your marriage in the way of healthy fighting. We all struggle in this area and need to continually be subjecting our wills, pride, and stubbornness to the lordship of Jesus.

Write in your Workbook #39. What are some Healthy Fighting Rules you have developed as a couple that help your marriage? What are some patterns that have developed that are hurting your marriage? What Healthy Fighting Rules can you decide on together that will have lasting benefits on your marriage?

Figure Out Your Hurt

When thinking about an issue you want to discuss with your husband, try to understand where you are really coming from. If the issue is pretty significant and may provoke you to tears, pay attention. Realize there is some significant pain in that area. Remind yourself that the level of pain you have about a particular issue is often rooted in your past hurt. It may actually have a root cause that is unrelated to the situation at hand. Get very curious about your heart as you are dealing with the issue. Somewhere, there is a hurt, disappointment, or expectation that is causing your current pain.

Bedroom Talk is Sacred

Everything goes into the bedroom. The day's stress, emotions, unforgiveness, insecurities, thoughts, and much more. Your conversations with your hubby *about* your intimacy definitely follow you into the bedroom. Jesus can heal and help you forgive and forget your past and the hurts you've done to each other. But, do not use that as a pass to say whatever you want to your husband about your sex lives. On a daily basis, our husband should be treated with deep value in every area. Your default posture towards him should be respect and tenderness, but especially in regards to sex. Bedroom talk is sacred. Do you remember the verse about the depth of sexual immorality? "All other sins a person commits are outside the body, but whoever sins sexually, sins against their own body" (1 Cor 6:18). On the flip side, holy sexual acts go just as deeply. How you and your husband regard sex affects one of the deepest parts of yourselves. Therefore communication around it should also have some protection. Three Bedroom Talk Laws every marriage should maintain when talking about sex. 1-Stay positive and compliment first; 2-Talk with "I" statements, not accusations; and 3-Be *very* gentle. Let me explain each of these and why you should incorporate these Bedroom Talk Laws.

Bedroom Talk Laws:

1- Stay Positive & Compliment First

Over the years I've noticed something, and it is backed up with scientific research.e generally remember the very first and last things we hear and maintain a more vague sense of the middle content. The first things mentioned set the tone and expectations for the rest of the conversation. It also provides a vision for how the conversation to flow. Start respectfully, infuse with appreciation, and include a vision of the direction you ultimately would like the conversation to move. I have a wonderfully sensitive husband whose facial expressions show many of his thoughts. He is still very reserved in sharing his feelings, but I can generally sense if he's disappointed or if what I've said hurt him. This helps me to remember to be kind in my words. If you can't read your husband's face like this, it means you have to work a little harder to remind yourself not to use cutting or hurtful words. Whether he shows it or not, they *do* affect. He probably doesn't share them openly with many people. You should be the number one person with whom he is open.

Can you imagine the rage you would feel if someone tramples on your husband's vulnerable heart? How angry you would be if someone makes him feel desperate, ashamed, belittled, or humiliated? It can create rage in me like no other when someone has perpetrated my hubby this way. We often forget that our own words can do that very thing to the person we love the most. We should *be* the safe place. Consider yourself as a soldier guarding your husband's emotions. There should be warmth and comfort in your embrace. You should protect and guard his heart, if he is generous enough to share. Every word you say that is cutting and mean-spirited tells him that you are not a safe haven and he should keep his feelings to himself or go elsewhere. Obviously in the context of the marriage bedroom, this is utterly important.

Start off by ensuring you both are at an emotionally good place. Consider what is going on with him and ask your husband if he has some time to talk or go walking. This ensures he's at a place mentally and emotionally where he can be present with you. Timing is important. If it is not the right time, he could receive your words badly, simply because of everything else going on. Try to be sensitive to that. Begin your conversation by reminding him of how much you love and appreciate him. This is a good beginning. It assures him of your love and devotion to him are *not* at question here. Then move onto a relevant compliment of him in the bedroom. For example, if I wanted to talk to D about wanting him to initiate sex more often in the bedroom. I may start by saying, "Honey, do you mind if I talk to you about something? I love you so much and am excited because I feel like our love-making is really exciting for me, especially recently".

Write in your Workbook #40. Think of something you'd like to talk to your husband about regarding the marriage bed. How can you start the conversation with positivity and compliments? Write a possible example here.

2- Talk in I-Statements, Not Accusations

When approaching your husband, remember the issue you have is *your* issue. Here's an illustration. When a man opens a door for a woman, he could be doing it for a million different reasons. It is the woman's interpretation that determines her response to it. Based on her past experiences, a woman could think the man is opening the door a) because he thinks she's incapable of doing it herself; b) he wants to sleep with her and thinks this is a good segway into a conversation; c) he wants her to feel respected and valued as a woman; d) he wants to look her over as she walks in front of him; or e) he feels that she may be going through a lot and could use a kind gesture. All of those different interpretations originated in her own mind. There's a slew more of possible reasons, but her appreciation or offense is dependent solely on *her*. It's *her* interpretation of the event and *her* issue.

Putting this in perspective of your own marriage, when you are upset about something in the bedroom, it is *your* issue. It is not a fact. It is not truth. It is *your* interpretation of an event. Just because it is your issue does not mean it doesn't need to be talked about. But owning it instead of accusing is best. You may even be right in your interpretation; but assuming that before asking has a negative impact on the conversation. Using "I" statements helps to diffuse, where an accusation ignites. Continuing our example, if the woman has a negative interpretation of his motives, she could accuse "Don't treat me like a weakling. I can do it myself!" Can you imagine how this could offend the man who just wanted to do an act of kindness for this woman? Instead, realizing it is her interpretation (that may even be wrong), she could say apologetically "I have a problem with people opening the door for me. It makes me feel like they think I'm incapable." This gives the man the benefit of the doubt and lets him know honestly how she's feeling. Let the default of your marriage be to give the benefit-of-the-doubt.

Talking in "I" statements, also models the vulnerability you'd like to happen on both sides in the conversation. Accusing words naturally are responded to with defensiveness. Defensiveness typically moves into self-justification. Instead, you want to have a conversation with your hubby that encourages him to bear his soul in order for true openness and change to occur. To come back to my example, with my husband, if I use accusatory words like "You never initiate sex with me." What options does he have except, "Yes I do. Remember when..." or worse, "Well, that's because you..."? Instead I could say, "I love it when you approach me to make love. It makes me feel that you really desire me. Do you think you could do that tonight, when I don't expect it? I especially like when you begin by caressing my back and telling me how my body makes you feel. I would love that even more often, maybe every couple of days. What do you think?"

Write in your Workbook #41. Going back to the conversation you began scripting above, write a dialogue of exactly what you could say to him using "I" statements.

3- Be Very Gentle

This should be your default posture when planning to talk about sex. Remind yourself how deeply your man appreciates the sex act. It is not a whim, but a deep-seated heart desire for you to love the sex you share with him. One of the worst feelings for a man is not feeling good enough. Just as a woman wants to be cherished, a man wants to feel like he's fully capable. You have the opportunity to guard that part of his heart in your marriage. He is indeed good enough. He is proficient and powerful.

If you haven't read much about the male psyche, it is an investment in your marriage's health and happiness. Wild at Heart, Love & Respect, Love & War, and Every Man's Battle are great reads for the learning wife. But a central desire of your man is to feel like he is part of a grand adventure, the warrior saving the day. You have the opportunity to protect and honor this ambition. Also, *you* are not his God-given adventure. You are his partner in the adventure. As wise wives, we have to sometimes get out of the way and be a faithful companion. We have to resist the urge to be an attention-seeking, drama-hungry, or egoistic princess. Ask God to show you if you need to die to yourself in some areas to become balanced in your marriage. Because you are so close to your husband, you have the opportunity to slash and belittle his dreams or uphold and honor them.

Just as you are his queen, he is your king. He should protect and cherish your precious heart and you should respect and honor his courageous and adventurous spirit. The bedroom has a lot to do with your husband's feelings of self worth. It is not the end-all be-all (though sometimes it feels like it to him), but it has the power to diminish enjoyment and focus from other areas of his life.

Men can get sex out of proportion in their head. Our society tells them if you're not constantly "getting it" they're not good enough. This is not God's truth. That is not our job to correct. Our job is to *love* our husbands and pray. Remember, love isn't self-seeking, prideful, easily angered, nor keeps a record of wrongs. Love is kind, patient, rejoicing in the truth; love always protects, trusts, hopes, perseveres, and never fails. So take *care* to be gentle and *love* him in your words.

Write in your Workbook #42. Revisiting the issue you're planning to discuss, are you being *loving* and gentle in your attitude and approach to him? Edit or rewrite the script here.

Cleaning Up

You may have to clean up the past a little bit. Sexual rejection can be more painful than most other kinds of rejection. You probably have gathered by now that I would highly recommend not making your husband feel ashamed or embarrassed by his sexual initiations. You don't want him to feel bad for this God-given desire (and that will not make it go away, it will just make him feel negatively towards you). His libido is working *for* your marriage. It is vital. As you remember your rejections of his advances, have you been loving, kind, and gentle? You may need to make some changes.

It is important to realize he deserves respect even when the answer is "no". He is not a dog requesting crumbs from the table. He is your honorable husband, asking his sexy wife--that he just cannot resist--if she would spend some love and energy on him. Maybe it'll take an hour. If you fully engage, by the end you'll be glad you did! If you are not able or willing to make love at that moment, continue to treat him with the dignity. Take his advances as a compliment. Make sure you tell him how much you love him and let him down kindly. Something as simple as "You know I love you and want to make love to my sexy hubby, but I don't think I can right now. Mind if we go for it tomorrow?" Give him hope that your answer next time will be yes. Then it is your job to try to make sure it is (check out Prepare and Be Sexy section for tips here).

My aim is your default answer would become "yes." And you'll become comfortable initiating as well (whether you're in the mood or not, you know he is). More sex makes for a better marriage. Of course I mean "sex" as an experience fully enjoyed by the wife as well. He should generally feel encouraged to approach you. You should be excited by his advances. Be grateful. Your relationship is the highest priority. I have spoken to women who *wish* their husbands would approach them more. There are marriages on all ends of the spectrum. Men who demand it, men who are too timid to approach you, and men who have other things inhibiting them. Ask God to help you understand your husband and respect him.

Were there times that you shamed or made your husband feel embarrassed by coming on to you? If there have been experiences like this, it is time to apologize and change. We all make mistakes and maybe unconsciously you have wounded your husband in a serious way. Forgiveness is what is needed and the first step is to apologize. Everyone makes mistakes--if you are not, you're not growing. Ask for his forgiveness and let him know you appreciate his advances.

Write in your Workbook #43. Are you excited by your husband initiating sex? If not, why? a) Write out exactly the reasons behind your hesitancy or why you normally say "no". b) Spend time problem-solving. For example, if you usually are too tired, how can you shift your schedule, change your diet, or cancel less important commitments to make sure you have the energy to invest in this vital relationship. c) Ask God to change your heart and help you to be grateful in becoming closer to your husband through making love. Ask Him to help you sort through your hesitancies and heal you from any past experiences that tie into it.

Steamy To Do:
Send your hubby a steamy text midday. Take a scandalous picture giving him some enjoyable views (maybe cleavage or panties). Include "Can't wait to be with you tonight ;)".

Communicate Orally

Tell Him "Your Plan"

So, how do you talk to him specifically about peni? If you've been married for any length of time you have a certain pattern already developed that probably doesn't involve oral pleasure. Or since you've picked up this book, at least not to the extent to which you (and he) would like. With your Bedroom Talk Rules understood and practiced in your Workbook, let's talk to him about your plan. Using our formula, tell your husband how much you love him and are grateful for your marriage. Explain to him that you have been doing some reading about how you can be a better wife to him. Remember, you don't want him to feel condemned in any way (it's *your* issue that *you* want to get better at). Depending on your marriage, a little humor may be what the doctor ordered. I would encourage you to tell him about a book you're reading that is helping you to understand yourself and your sexuality more.

Talk About The Dream

Explain the dream you have of your marriage and your intimacy. Read to him what you wrote in your workbook about your 30 year goals for the two of you. If you haven't done so already and there are areas that you feel the conviction of the Holy Spirit to apologize, make sure you do that before you go any further. You could say, "Firstly, I know I haven't been perfect in our marriage. I know there are things I need to change and apologize for. But I am committed to moving forward towards this goal in our marriage". Ask him what he would like to see as your intimacy in 30 years. Listen carefully and ask questions if you are not fully understanding anything. Let him know that the book you're reading is specifically about orally pleasuring your husband.

Explain to him how your heart is changing and you're beginning to understand that this act is part of intimacy and as you learn to pleasure him, you'll really enjoy it too.

Explain Your Vulnerability

Explain to him that this is actually hard for you to talk about because it feels very vulnerable and even scary. This is probably not intuitive to him. He needs to know you feel like you're taking a risk to bring this up. He also needs to know that every time you take a risk in the bedroom you are fighting against fear. This will help him understand how gentle and encouraging he should be with you. You may want to insert some humor. You could say, "since I'm a newbie, I need you to be very positive, and encouraging". That will cue him into being gentle with you as you step out of your comfort zone. Ask him for help in this area. Let him know complimenting your efforts would be really helpful.

Ask Him for Help

As a note for wives, it is not a rip on your lovemaking abilities to try to improve. It is actually a sign of confidence to be able to recognize where you want to improve it. The masters in every field practice daily and use coaches all because they are constantly aiming towards improvement. The fact that you are trying to get better at lovemaking means you are well on your way, already. And it goes up from here!

Ask him if he'd be okay with you trying some new things out. Ask him if he would be encouraging and positive--without pressure--in the small risks you will be taking. Even more practically, I have found it really effective to ask my hubby point-blank to help train me in this. I'm not kidding. You want to be the best lover you can be. You want your hand to make him orgasm better than his own. This can only happen if he shows you the peculiarities of his own body. If you do not yet have the confidence level to bring this up, keep working the steps above. Slowly, as you begin to believe his love and appreciation of your sexuality and you grow in confidence, you'll be able to get to this place.

My husband is very reserved in telling me what he likes in bed. It takes a lot of maneuvering and safe-space-making for him to open up about this. It is surely worth my effort. As you learn one extra thing and implement it, you'll love to see the exhilaration and pleasure you get to provide. As you're learning, while doing the act, consider it a practice lesson. Be very clear and curious about his preferences and you will continue to get better and more able to pleasure him fully.

Thank him for being so good at listening and tell him how excited you are. His commitment to help and support you will be important. It means he understands this is vulnerable for you, but you're going to push through. Remind him lastly of the marriage and intimacy you are excited to have with him.

Some Things Can Remain Under Wraps

If your husband read this book, he may feel a little sick at how contrived and robotic I make, what "should be natural". Well, it's not natural for everyone for many reasons. We can get to a place where it does feels that way. It didn't start that way for me, but now I feel like it is natural. Unfortunately, telling him all your mental processing may not help him to be turned on. There are plenty of things you can tell him and receive his help in feeling comfortable. But some things you can keep that to yourself or talk it through with a trusted girlfriend (preferably one who has also taken this course and understands where you're coming from). Some things are meant to remain a mystery for your husband's enjoyment.

To put this in perspective, when your husband was planning his proposal, I hope he didn't come to you with all his worries and fears. Hopefully he went to his guy friend to vent and ask for advice. Recognize there is a point where you want to keep some details under wraps as not to hinder his sexual enjoyment. Limit your openness about your mental processing around giving oral pleasure. What you do decide to share, remember what you say will stay with him during the act.

I remember in the early days, sharing with my husband that sometimes I get tired during orally pleasuring him. It has taken him a long time and me convincing for him to fully relax and enjoy. But I still suspect he worries about my tiredness in the act at times. Don't make this mistake. If he is concerned about anything during the act, it will hinder his pleasure and it will extend the time he takes to orgasm (we'll get into this more soon!). So, find that girlfriend who (while honoring your husband) you can share some of your inner processing.

Don't Get Discouraged

The enemy of course wants to discontinue any activity that will bring your marriage closer together. He knows how powerful a strong marriage can be for the Kingdom. You two are a united force. The enemy wants to tear that down at its roots. I want you to fortify your mind against the enemy's attacks. We've addressed a good amount of the possible discouragers. There are more, and there are some specific to your marriage. You will need the guidance of the

Holy Spirit to unearth some. Are there areas of this project that makes you feel discouraged or like you won't succeed?

Write those in your workbook. Write in your Workbook #44. Ask the Holy Spirit for His truth in these areas. Listen. Write what you believe God would respond to you for these concerns.

Have Fun

As your communication about sex increases and becomes a safer place, you'll start to enjoy talking to him. It's really a lot of fun. Many husbands fall right asleep after sex. Don't feel sad, this is natural. His energy has gone out with his semen and it's time to sleep. Funny enough, my husband's sports coach would tell the team not to make love the night before a big game, because he wanted to make sure they had all their energy for the tournament. Women do not respond this way generally. Sex can make both parties sleep better, but sometimes women need to wind down afterwards, whereas men are automatically exhausted. I'm lucky because my husband usually has a solid 5 minutes afterwards that he manages to remain awake. Something he actually started doing but now we both enjoy, is asking afterwards "What was your favorite part?" It's a great question to ask. We both get the pleasure of reliving those exciting moments. Also we learn what the other likes and can plan to do more of that next time. It's also a great opportunity to compliment the other person on the wonderful things you enjoyed. If your hubby can't spare those few minutes before bed, don't worry. It's also really exciting breakfast talk.

Steamy To Do:

At the end of your next intimate encounter, lay on his chest and ask "Honey, will you tell me about your favorite parts?" If he is timid to answer, go ahead and elaborate on the touches, visuals, and movements you really enjoyed. Be generous with your compliments of his lovemaking.

Speaking in Bed

Language *In* Lovemaking

Admittedly, this is a touchy subject. Sex is inherently vulnerable. If you and your husband have not yet developed a language and way to talk in your marriage bed, I encourage you to start. I give some ideas. As I mentioned, I use less direct language in this book because I don't know your past. I don't know what you've been through and language can be a powerful reminder of things we'd rather forget. Certain language can stir up painful or sinful memories. So, I've tried to use language that I hope will be neutral for you. I do not think you necessarily should use these words in the bedroom. Be free with your words and ways of expressing your sexual desire and experience with him. There are many words I use *exclusively* during our lovemaking. It helps me to feel confident, turned on, and free with my body. It even gives me a way to express myself in a much more sexual way than my normal, chaste persona. But you will never hear me utter them in any other scenario, I assure you. I'm not saying you have to use foul words. But, as you start feeling more comfortable, you may want to start experimenting with some language that you wouldn't normally. It can increase excitement and desire.

Sensual Talking Ideas

If you're tongue-tied in bed and everything you say seems to sound ridiculous or you can't manage to utter a single word, I've been there. I want to give you some practical ideas. You do not have to sound like those women in movies, you can sound loving and kind and make him feel like superman if you share with him your positive thoughts about him. You can adopt a sensual and confident tone in your voice that will help you feel more sexy while talking to him. Compliment your hubby. Share with him a sexy fantasy or thought you have about him. Tell your man how sexy, hot, and attractive you think his body is. Remind him of how he turns you on. While doing peni, make sure he knows how much you love his member, the way it feels, the way it smells, and the way it tastes.

Now is not the time to be worried about flattery or over-complimenting. If there is anyone you want to be turned on by, it's your husband. Feel free to give compliments freely. Share with him how much you desire to touch his body and feel him close to you. Tell him how much you like to see him turned on. Tell him how you love him touching you that way. Share with him how great it feels to have him inside of you. If he is doing something that you really like, let him know how good it makes you feel. Share with him a time when he touched you or did something that got you so hot. These not only increase his confidence, but help him to know how to love you and your body better. Don't hesitate. It may feel uncomfortable in the beginning. Keep in mind: it is better to say something when needed, than not say anything because you weren't sure it's not perfect. The only way to get better is by *doing*. Focus on your purpose: To make him feel like a king and help both of you enter into a fantastic experience together. You will never graduate to saying the "right" things, if you don't start by saying *some* things. It will get easier and you will feel better. Eventually, you'll be surprised you had any hesitation at all. Don't be scared to practice your language and tone in the bathroom beforehand. This will help you to feel more confident and comfortable . If you have the right heart, to encourage and love on your husband, the words will flow. Let them.

Speak In Faith

Here's a wife's secret. I want my husband to turn me on more than anyone else. I want him to be the apple of my eye in *every* way. I want to be able to ignore every other man and only see my husband. And you know what? Thank God I am pretty much there. Having a sordid past of sexual sin made this originally a challenge, but God is gracious and has slowly redeemed my eyes and mind to have eyes just for him. What used to be a discipline to keep my mind aligned has become almost effortless. When I'm watching a movie with my single friends who comment on how attractive a certain actor is, I genuinely cannot see it. I usually comment "he seems ok, but he's not like D." I am so enraptured with my husband: his looks, his ways, his personality. As I approach him, seeing him at a distance excites my senses. I want to encourage you, dear sister, if the feelings of attraction for your husband have faded, keep the hope. This can not only return, but come stronger than ever before.

I am including this in the language section because our language has a powerful effect on our mind. As you are contemplating what and how you would like to speak to your husband in the bedroom, do not be afraid to speak in faith. Say what you're starting to feel and the feeling grows. Say even what you want to feel. Trust that the feeling will grow. I very much encourage you to say some of your lovemaking language in faith. It is not a pretense, it's the way I've found my mind and body works. From my research, I am not alone. Women, generally, need to commit their minds to lovemaking and their bodies respond to that commitment [4]. You are in love with your husband, whether you feel it or not. By faith you are making love because you know that will produce more love and unity between you both. It is not untruthful for you to act turned on as the feelings grow to match those actions.

Just as it is not untruthful for you to make your hubby coffee in the morning even though you are working through some upset feelings you have towards him from the day before. As women we often need to jumpstart our bodies by suggesting what we may be beginning to feel. Ever noticed if you ask a child on their way to the amusement park if they are excited, they are always so excited. This sets them up to have a great day. Your excitement, enthusiasm, and positivity of the event is an asset to great lovemaking. Do not shy away from this, it will create an environment of expectation and will allow your love to grow.

Faking It

Speaking or acting in faith as I encourage throughout this course is different than 'faking it'. 'Faking it' means to pretend to orgasm. This is *not* a helpful practice. Please do not pretend to orgasm with your husband. It is not fair to him and it is not fair to you. If you have done this in the past, you need to stop. If this is happening, the truth will be very hard for your husband to handle; it will deeply affect his confidence in the bedroom. I would suggest discontinuing the practice. Let him know you are having trouble coming to orgasm and you would like his help so you can get to this place. Through reading and self-discovery, I am confident you will get to this place. Orgasm is not something you should pretend to do 'in faith'.

Pretending to have an orgasm robs you and your husband of truly enjoying this joy and unifying experience. Instead of bringing the both of you together through sex, faking it drives a wedge of dishonesty between you both. Bringing his wife to orgasm is a discipline of patience, research, and selflessness that your husband can and should learn. But if he thinks he is already there, he's believing lies about your body which is pushing him farther from truly understanding you. It is a process of learning that can be very enjoyable and have rewards on every part of your relationship. You are fully capable of learning in your own body, figure out ways that you can orgasm in your marriage bed with hand stimulation and other practices that you and he should learn about.

God-fearing Seductress

Though a friend of mine is an extraordinary actress, she explained to me that she feels really awkward approaching her husband to make love. She feels like it's his job. Further, she feels like she isn't being godly in seducing him. She'll just tell him "we should have sex," in a timid and serious way. I am grateful that she realizes that sex needs to happen in her marriage. Every time you initiate does not have to include candles and a feather boa, but I encourage you to take the time to build anticipation and seduce him. The way my husband approaches me for sex has a big influence on how much I enjoy the experience. If he goes first for my most sensitive areas and ignores every other part of my body, I have a hard time getting into the experience. But if he first of all gives my face, lips, and neck attention, then caresses my arms, breasts, and abdomen, by the time he moves further south I am so much more engaged and ready to enjoy.

Many Christian women miss that you can be sexy and God-fearing. Just because you love Jesus doesn't mean you do not take care to seduce your husband. Your husband would love your playful, fun, or sexy seduction. Thinking of your husband's likes and desires will help to guide you in turning him on. Free yourself to be a God-fearing seductress. Your husband loves being seduced by you. Remember, God made your hubby's equipment to respond to your enticing form.

Another reason a wife passes up seduction because she doesn't want to feel exposed to rejection or negative judgments. Realize your husband craves this part of intimacy. When you provide a little show or sensual visual for him, he can draw you to mind later in the day or week when he is tempted by some other stimuli. You can load him up with images and experiences that will satisfy and help him to avoid temptations. Keep things interesting. What pleasures or tricks did you find he really enjoyed in the early days? Maybe it's time to pull those back out.

Practice By Yourself First

As I mentioned, I don't believe pleasuring your husband is something that comes naturally. For some, I guess it does. Not for me. Nothing with sex has come "naturally". Each area that I feel comfortable with now started in a very uncomfortable and vulnerable practice. Consider yourself blessed if this not your story. But if it is, there is *hope*. You will not always have to struggle in your mind to find the words, the body gestures, the areas that turn on yourself or your husband. But it may start out that way. Here's what I suggest. Practice by yourself. Lock yourself in the bathroom and visualize every moment of your sexual experience. Practice (out loud) your words and compliments about his body, how it tastes, and how it feels. Practice the seductive tone of your voice. Also, practice your facial expressions. Keep in mind, the point is to give your husband a wonderful experience and if you really want to get good, practice is the key.

Steamy To Do:

By yourself, in front of your full-length mirror, imagine you are seducing your husband. Put on some music. Run your hands up your legs and give the mirror an enticing expression. Believe your body is sexy and desirable, and work it!

SECTION V

Love His

Member

Most Important Understanding

I've been fairly easy with my imagery thus far, but I must warn you the following is not for the unwed eyes. I will aim to be tasteful, but it is important we do not miss the understanding because of flowery language. I want you to walk away from this course with as much practical application as possible.

Your husband needs to feel that you treasure and value him. In the act of peni, you can provide honor to him as a man. When you get this piece right, your entire sex life will move to another level. By mastering the keys to give amazing head you will...

1) feel fully confident in your understandings of his arousal and your abilities to bring him pleasure,

2) understand how he sees you and what about you turns him on,

3) model service and selflessness in the marriage bed,

4) have a safe space for both of you to share more openly about sexual desires,

5) give him and yourself a lot of pleasure and fun, and

6) possess a foundation of marital generosity, providing for endless enjoyment and discovery.

He Loves Receiving This Gift

Many men enjoy felatio as much or more than penetration. If this surprises you, I am glad you're reading this book! Aside from it feels good, here are some of the major reasons for this.

A) You're In Command- He can relax and let you take charge. Cultural norms tell men they are responsible for the sex act. They are the ones who need to do all the work in bed and if the woman doesn't enjoy, it is his fault. This is a lot of pressure on him. Many men suffer from performance anxiety for this reason--and it is a major reason for erectile dysfunction (more on this later). It is nice for him to sit back and just enjoy.

B) Visual- Depending on your position, giving head provides him with very gratifying views of your curves, backside, face, and cleavage. All of which are incredibly pleasing to his eyes. Don't you dare turn off the lights! Let him fully indulge in this visual feast.

C) Being Served- Just as we all enjoy being doted on, it is especially enjoyable for his wife to consider his likes and deliver accordingly. It is also a wonderful joy for you to know what makes him go wild and bring him effectively to orgasm.

D) No Risk of Pregnancy- Depending on the season of your marriage, he may enjoy this sexual activity that has no risk of pregnancy. Condoms can constrict and other forms of contraceptives do have low failure rates, but they may provide an ounce of worry for him. Receiving head does not carry that concern. It is also an activity that can be enjoyed shortly after giving birth, during yeast infections, and at other times when sex is not an option.

E) Feels Great- Your warm, wet, and soft lips loving on his member is unlike any other feeling. You have the ability to give him pleasure like *nothing* else. Intercourse of course is phenomenal and other intimate options are too, but your mouth and tongue provide a variety of unique and wonderful pleasures for your man.

F) Male Dominance- This is something you may not be very keen on at first, but I will try to explain. Some men really enjoy this act specifically because it makes them feel powerful. When his wife is on her knees serving him, he feels like he is 'has it all': an incredible wife who loves him and serves him selflessly. I love my sensitive, humble, and patient husband. Though he is not the talkative or in-your-face type, when we're in the bedroom I aim to make him feel like a king. I know my honey and I know this greatly matters to him. I love that there is something I can do to make him feel so significant and powerful. Imagine what that does for his confidence, self-esteem, and feelings towards me. (You can always flip this around and remember that you actually have all the power. You can provide intense pleasure or pain at your will). His feeling like a king does not debase you in any way. When D is generous in this way with me, considering exactly what I like and making me feel like a queen, it makes me value and cherish him more. It is the same when you serve your man orally.

G) Feel Wanted/Sexy- Your response to his member during oral makes him feel wanted. He feels that you like his body and his most important part. It shows him how much you are physically turned on by him. It shows him how much you love him.

H) Honoring His Essence- The penis is the defining feature of a man. I will explain more soon. Realize this act of love touches his deepest emotional parts. When my husband holds me and listens to me through tears and vulnerability, I feel loved in the deepest place. Take a minute to consider a time you have felt deeply loved by your husband. Now realize that doing peni for your husband may give him that level of fulfillment.

Importance To Your Husband

He desires you to approach him and give him oral. Including your previous rejections, he has probably struggled with the understanding that the desire for receiving head is bad or improper. These unmet urges may have pushed him at least to feel ashamed and embarrassed. Many men truly feel pained that their wives won't happily do this for them. (Remember how forgotten special occasions affect you.) They have probably tried to kill the desire for receiving this from their wives. Furthermore, through his life, your husband has been told that penis size is the end-all-be-all to satisfying a woman.

As a side: this is a horrible marketing ploy to sell pumps and pills. It's very sad because it makes men feel inadequate and helpless. It is also ridiculous, because it is scientifically unfounded. A bigger penis does not mean better sex. The vast majority of women cannot orgasm through penetration only. They require clitoral stimulation first and foremost (sometimes nothing else). The clitorous is situated outside of the vagina, so really the portion just above the penis, his hands, and method of thrusting provides more pleasure for her than a large penis ever could. Women whose husbands are too large for her physical comfort is actually a bigger problem.

Back to my earlier point: men are very nervous about their penis, the shape of their testicles, the shrinkage when flaccid, the semen taste, and appearance. He hates not feeling good enough especially in the area of sex. You have the opportunity to tenderly affirm and ease his fears.

Remember his member is not the same as his hand, ear or foot. It's the essence of his manhood. Your regard for his member has a deep impact on him. He has treasured that thing since boyhood. He happened upon its sensitivity in infancy. He learned how to point and aim in urinals and behind trees. He has protected it through junior high's football games. He deeply values his member and he *wants* you to do the same. His desire for your oral appreciation has a godly fulfillment in marriage.

MOST IMPORTANT: Your Attitude

Consider again, the sensual, virtuous, and holy wife in Song of Solomon enjoying her husband's fruits. Song of Songs 2:3 "Like an apple tree among the trees of the forest is my beloved among the young men. I delight to sit in his shade, and his fruit is sweet to my taste." Notice the wife's attitude. She delights to taste her husband's fruits. This is pivotal in giving your husband amazing pleasure. When Solomon heard these words his heart probably leapt with joy. Since that was her attitude, it probably wasn't really a surprise because she made him feel that it was her delight.

Is this the way you see your husband's package? Do you delight to be near it? Do you enjoy the taste and all the other senses involved in kissing and sucking on it? Do you feel excited to have the opportunity to enjoy his fruits? This is exactly how this virtuous wife of the Bible felt about her husband. You have the opportunity to feel the same way about your husband. I say this a pivotal understanding because everything else flows out of it. If you believe your husband's penis is wonderful, fun, and something you cannot get enough of, you will feel confident in discovering and experimenting. But if you feel unsure if you enjoy his member, then you will be wrought with fear and insecurities.

Notice the sensual wife of Song of Solomon: "with great pleasure" she gave her husband head." As an honoring wife, she didn't just "do her duty". She took *great* pleasure in what she was doing. She enjoyed tasting his fruits. What does it look like to love his member? When you love it, you feel comfortable around it. You want to touch and pleasure it. You enjoy caressing and teasing it. You like to cop a feel when he doesn't expect. You get excited to find out new ways to make it hard. It brings *you* pleasure to make it feel good. This is a pivotal piece. You love his member. This is the attitude that gives him an amazing experience.

How Would You Feel?

Let's see things from his perspective. Consider for a moment how intimate and important your vulva is. Imagine your husband going down on you. But, when he approaches your most intimate area, you can sense his hesitancy. He looks uncomfortable, nervous, or even disgusted. Worse yet, because it is so pleasurable to you, you asked him for it--but he makes it look like a chore. Talk about horrifying. Imagine how that experience would affect the way you feel about him outside of the bedroom. In contrast, imagine your husband is *totally* in love with your genital womanhood. He begins to caresses your breasts, waist, thighs and butt. His face shows excitement as he continues down your body. He kisses all around your pubic area so gently. He teases your vulva lips lightly. Then he slowly and tenderly begins kissing and licking your clitorous with such skill and passion. All the while, he tells you how much he loves your "flower" and it's beauty. You can relax as you trust he completely enjoys giving and bringing you utter ecstasy. This would be an incredible experience for you would it not? Wouldn't it also positively affect every other part of your relationship?

Write in your Workbook #45. Write down some of the things you would like your husband to say about seeing, smelling, and tasting your lady parts? How would you like his face to look when looking at your womanhood? How would you like him to feel about your most intimate parts?

Perspective Shifting

If you have gone for it in the past, good for you! Please be encouraged to go for it again. If you fumbled before, no problem. Your husband is thrilled that you want to get great at giving head. As you may have guessed by now, not all orgasms are the same. Women generally need everything *just right* in order to have an orgasm. Your husband is less picky and will be able to orgasm even under less than ideal circumstances. But, just because he came, does not mean he doesn't feel disappointment. Maybe you were hesitant before. Maybe you weren't sure entirely what to do and felt awkward. Maybe you thought it was nasty or accidentally made it seem gross or like a chore. I'm sorry to tell you, but, your husband is just as aware during the act as any other time of the day. He can sense your hesitation. He can sense that you're not comfortable being near his member. He may not have stopped you because that would have made it worse (or made you feel bad). And he still wanted you to try because it feels so great. If you were half-hearted or felt like it was an actual job, remember how *you* would feel. If he did that to you, you would feel less loved--not more. Everything shows on your face. Every thought you have about his penis *shows*.

Go Ahead & Apologize

If this is where you are, think about the following. Saying a simple "I'm sorry" can break down walls. It can heal hurts that may be years old. It is easy to say, but we do not say it nearly as often as we should. Just because you made a mistake in the past or didn't know any better doesn't make you a failure. It makes you human. *Everyone* makes mistakes. You are in the process of learning. Most people don't grow enough even to recognize something they did was a mistake. You should feel proud of yourself; you're ahead of the curve. If you are not making mistakes, you are not growing. Please, for the sake of your marriage, always be *quick* to apologize. For example, say "Honey, I want you to know that I am sorry for making you feel uncomfortable when I have gone down on you before. I was insecure and I didn't know how that made you feel. I am learning to really love peni. When the time is right, would you mind if I try again?"

Write in your Workbook #46. What will you say to your husband about the state of where things are? How you will say you are sorry? Write out exactly what you will say.

Decision Time

To reiterate: he'd *love* your oral attention if done right. I don't mean "done right" by having great technique and skill (though that will make you feel more confident). I mean you give head "right" by having the right opinion of his member. The first step to "delight" in his fruits is to make a decision. How completely "unsexy" right? But I am very serious. You need to decide to love your husband's member. Commit to yourself that you are going to *love* all of his shaft, head, glans, frenulum...the whole "apple tree". (If there are specific reasons--ie: hygiene, hair, past experience etc.--you are having trouble loving it, check out some possible solutions in Troubleshooting section).

Decide to love your husband's member. Decide that you cannot wait to touch, tease, and suck on it. Am I asking you to pretend? Not exactly--it may feel like you're pretending in the beginning. But as I have encouraged many times so far, push through the discomfort. It will feel unusual and uncomfortable at first. That is normal. Press through those feelings. Choose to love his most treasured part. This is not something you can do half-heartedly. You need to commit to love it and keep committing your mind to it. Act like you love it and say that you do. Remember: doing peni on him means *loving* your husband. Love, as you'll remember, isn't self-seeking, proud, easily angered, it keeps no records of wrongs and it never fails. Love is patient, kind, rejoicing in the truth, always hopes, trusts, protects and *perseveres*.

The Reward

You stick with this. You *decide* to love your husband--all of him--and pretty soon, you'll start feeling the love for his extra special part. It starts to be something that you can't wait to play with, touch, and arouse. You can't wait to suck on it when he is unsuspecting. This was not automatic for me. I had to work on committing myself to love it. But after seeing how I could give great pleasure to my husband, how deeply he appreciated my excitement, and how fun love making became, it actually became very pleasurable for me also. It has become a sense of pride that I have the power to completely arrest his thoughts and cause him to feel such powerful enjoyment at my will.

At risk of giving too much information I'll share an experience with you (we're basically sisters by now, right?). The other day, D was on the phone sitting on the bed. I could tell he was getting a little frustrated by whatever was being said. (It wasn't serious just annoying miscommunications). Without a word, I pulled aside his shorts and started teasing him. He tried to resist, but with a sexy smile, I persisted. (I *knew* he loved it). Listening to him stumble over his words and try desperately to end the conversation, was really exciting to me. He was able to hang up the phone pretty quickly and we had a *lot* of fun. Did I start out excited (or even turned on)? No. But because I really love his member, supported by many experiences, I feel free to act that way. By committing to and fully participating in that act, I found myself incredibly turned on and ready for whatever happened next. My body physically responded to me fully enjoying giving him pleasure.

Whether you feel it or not, love his member. The rewards are just around the corner, not just for your husband, your marriage, but also yourself!

Steamy To Do:

While your hubby is shaving in front of the mirror, brush your teeth over the sink and give him a sensual surprise. Wearing just your underwear, bend over to seductively rub your backside on his front. Give him a playful smile.

How His Member Works

Be Curious

Begin to get curious when you notice something happening through his shorts; what may be happening in his mind? Get interested in what specifically turns him on. Become very curious about how his member works. We are going to go into specifics. Throughout, remember that your husband is unique. What works for most, what is scientifically accurate about many, may be unique for your husband. Also, realize there may be reasons your husband does not like things that *should* be pleasurable. There may be insecurities in his mind from some past understanding or experiences that may make him wary of certain activities. Be sensitive to those and *respect* them. Remember this is all for his pleasure. It is not your job to change him. Do not to take anything personally. Depending on how adept your husband is at saying things kindly, you might have to develop a thick skin; let things that could be hurtful just roll off your back. Realize you are approaching a sensitive issue when approaching oral sex (yes, pun intended). It is probably a sensitive area for you both, because it touches some of your insecurities of being a good enough lover. Push through your discomfort and try to understand his perspective and care for his needs. Remember, peni is about *him*. Be the person who actively loves *first*. Set the example. As he heals and enjoys, it may simultaneously provide insight and healing for you. Be patient, kind, generous, and curious.

Anatomy Lesson

Very practically speaking, it is important to understand the various particular sensitive areas on your man. Understanding the different parts and how they work, will give you a greater confidence as you begin the journey to master oral sex. Get curious! Starting from the bottom:

Perineum - Literally the bottom. Just between his anus and his scrotum is a sensitive, soft skin that can be very pleasurable to the touch. It also depends on your man. He may consider that too close to the anus and be uncomfortable with touching there. (Also note, though it is not the subject of this book, the anus and prostate, hidden just inside, can be incredibly pleasurable for men with the courage to discover that area as well.) Learn what your husband enjoys, but hopefully he'll allow you to gently stroke this sensitive area.

Scrotum - aka ball sac. This sac is holding your hubby's testicles (plural: testes, aka balls) where millions of semen are created and stored. It is very sensitive and your man may enjoy you to tickle them. Using your fingers, lightly caress, and fondle them. You can lightly pinch the scrotal skin. Be careful not to pinch the testes themselves, they feel pain very easily. While you're in the area, use your mouth to kiss and gently suck on them. No need to have both in your mouth at the same time; that could really hurt him. Just be gentle, but generous with his jewels. Fyi: some men do not like these touched at all. Try it gently and discover your hubby's preferences.

Shaft - The part of the penis known as the "shaft" is the cylinder that extends from his body just before the head. This fills with blood, becoming elongated and erect during arousal. It is much less sensitive and can withstand (and enjoy) much more pressure than any other part of the penis. Even teasing (but gentle) bites may be welcome on this area.

Underside of Shaft- When looking at your husband's erect penis, this is the bottom of his shaft (the portion facing the ground). From the base to the head is a soft area in which the urethra tube runs. This is the tube that carries the semen from the scrotum to the tip when ejaculating. A firm lick from base to tip on the underside of the shaft can be especially pleasurable.

Glans or Head- Generally considered the most erogenous part of the penis. The glans is highly concentrated with nerve endings. There are many similarities to the glans and the clitoris anatomically. On uncircumcised men, the foreskin covers the head completely when flaccid keeping it wet and protected within. When erect the foreskin fully contracts and looks the same as an erect uncircumcised penis. On both circumcised and uncircumcised men, the penis head is incredibly sensitive and should be treated with care.

Corona or Rim- This is the area of the glans or head that slightly overhangs the shaft. If you imagine the glans as the top of a mushroom, the rim is the edge around the circumference of the mushroom. It is another of the most touch-receptive areas of the penis. Stimulating just this border of the head with your tongue is quite gratifying.

Frenulum- This is the unique elastic band of tissue at the end of the Underside of Shaft the penis. The Frenulum connects the shaft to the foreskin and/or head, located on the underside. From underneath the penis, it looks like a "Y" shape. This specific part is the most sensitive part of the penis. Give special attention to the Frenulum but realize you don't want to stimulate excessively too early on (consider how you feel about the clitorous stimulated too early).

Erection Understandings

The average man experiences eleven full or partial erections daily [1]. This would be an interesting question for your hubby, but chances are he experiences far more than you would imagine. It is important to realize every time he is erect is not necessarily because of a sexual thought or desire. It is actually a way his body cleans itself. In other parts of the body, blood is constantly flowing and cleaning areas of normal metabolic waste. But a flaccid penis does not receive this constant blood flow [2]. Frequent erections clean out the penis for health purposes. As a sensual wife, it is helpful to know there are four different reasons for your husband's erections. 1) Sometimes something, even an inanimate object, brushing up against his penis creates a reflex erection. 2) Psychogenic erections are inspired by a sexual thought or visual exciting him. 3) There is the biological morning erection aka nocturnal penile tumescence [3]. 4) The spontaneous erection that is unexpected, but also a natural phenomenon for your husband.

If your husband is having trouble becoming erect (many different factors play into this, including physical health, confidence, or stress---to name a few) utilizing any erection for sex is a great idea. No matter how it came about, it can certainly be used for sex. An exciting sexual experience in the morning can provide him mental visuals and images throughout the day which will help provide desire and encourage more sex. Getting him out of a slump is the best way to move forward. If you haven't done much morning sex, now is the time. Just waking up is a great time for sex also because testosterone levels are generally higher in the morning and decrease as the day wears on. The stressors and concerns of life aren't on his mind early in the morning, so he'll be able to enjoy the experience more.

These are helpful guides because if your man is stressed, distracted, or depressed the psychogenic erections may not be as easy for him. For example, if your husband does not become erect (though he certainly enjoys) watching you undress, you can begin stimulating him for a reflex erection. Do not to go straight for sucking, stroking, and stimulating his glans. Instead, happily tease, touch, lightly squeeze, and nibble on his shaft to get him excited to feel your mouth around his whole member.

Steamy To Do:

Plan morning passion. Set your alarm clock for a half hour earlier and ensure your designated day would be good for his schedule too. Once you wake, do whatever you need to do to feel fresh early in the morning (ie: brush teeth, hair, and wash face). Then begin kissing his neck and lips. Begin to disrobe him as he slowly wakes up. Give him some kind "good mornings" and keep things moving for an exciting romp before breakfast.

Great Oral (aka Peni) Starts in HisMind

What is Sexy

When preparing your mind to approach your husband, consider what types of teasing, caressing, or language will excite his senses. Just because you're married to this man, doesn't mean you rob him of the fun and enjoyment of being seduced. Yes, he knows you intimately. That means you can play and have fun with him when you're acting as a temptress. It's a safe place to experiment with your favorite sexy accents, verbiage, costumes, and sexy performances. Why not let your husband enjoy a little show? Get your nerve up and be willing to give him a sexy chair dance. Selecting a nice piece of music to accompany your show will help you and him to relax and have fun. He will love your willingness to spice things up and go out on a limb for his pleasure. I'd encourage you to practice by yourself first. This will help you to feel more at ease during. Practice being confident. Practice feeling confident while performing.

Your husband enjoys seeing your body. He enjoys seeing you in sexy clothes. He loves your curves. He chose you to marry and who you are is very attractive to him. Visuals that do nothing for you are incredibly enjoyable to him. Remember: confidence *is* sexy. Just as men have to decide to be confident about their penis size (something they can't do a darn thing about), it's not about the size, shape, or perk of your body. It's really about what you confidently do with it. Don't sell yourself short, your body is hot and your husband would *love* to see you doing something risque just to please him!

Element of Mystery

There is always an element of mystery to sexual desire. The guarded woman may be cold and harmful--hiding wounds that need light and love to heal. That is not what I mean when I encourage being mysterious. If you have areas of deep pain that you have not shared with your husband, other trusted friends and God, honor those. Be honest and allow God to heal those areas. By going through this process, you can get to a place of wholeness. You will then have the power to be a fully aware, healed, and confident woman.

However, a whole yet mysterious woman in the bedroom is intriguing and enticing. Your husband doesn't need to know *all* of your mind. Don't admit to him how silly you feel. Don't ask him if you look stupid. Or melt into a pile of jello the moment he gazes upon you in lingerie. Linger in the doorway wearing your scandalous teddy. Sometimes, you have to flaunt it before you feel it. Sometimes, you have to pretend to be confident, even when you don't feel confident. As Joyce Meyer says, you often just have to "do it, afraid". We all feel silly and even ridiculous before we feel strong and confident. Put on a face of fearlessness and go for it.

I remember being terrified of eating in restaurants. I came from a large family of humble means, we would eat at a restaurant, at the most, one time per year. Every occasion we did, my mother used it as a teaching moment. Napkins in laps, elbows off the table, and we *dare not* speak with our mouths full. In high school, I began interning at a professional office. Every day, my boss would take me and the other professionals out for lunch. I was practically sweating each day by 11:30 am anticipating the noontime meal. I knew I'd need to engage in appropriate small talk, act relaxed when picking up the correct spoon, and dabbing my mouth gingerly with the napkin which was otherwise in my lap. Inside I was so scared I'd drip something on my blouse or I'd accidentally chime into the conversation while my mouth was full. Years later I realized that no one was sitting judging my performance. There was no reason to be scared. The others were all too concerned with their own meals and the conversation to be evaluating how I was handling the situation. This is true in the bedroom as well. Your husband is delighted at the sight of you and your effort to entice him. Everything feels awkward the first few times. Push through the discomfort and you will end up satisfying your hubby and enjoying a marriage better than you may have dreamed.

Switch Things Up

As I alluded, every now and then I like to give my hubby an intimate treat. Yes, we have our more routine love making which is enjoyable for both of us. We have kind of figured out what works for both of us to feel fulfilled. But, to ensure we continue to have a vital and strong sexual intimacy, I insert some spicy experiences to keep things interesting every couple of days or weeks. My goal is to keep him intrigued and even guessing. I also really enjoy the thrill of these new treats and it keeps things fresh and exhilarating for me as well. If I am not taking risks in our intimacy, it's easy to fall into a routine that starts to feel nice but eventually a little stale. We need to be careful to keep our sex life fun and exciting for both our husbands and ourselves. As sex expert Dr. Ian Kerner says, "variety isn't just the spice of life; it's the very life blood of great sex" [4].

I brainstorm things which I can do for him that are unexpected or surprising. Consider how loved you feel (or would feel) with the random surprises your husband does for you, ie: flowers, rubbing your back in the kitchen, leaving a love note for you, cleaning the house, or giving you a surprise back massage. Your effort of creativity infuses your marriage with surprise and fresh zeal that helps you both stay engaged, excited, and passionate.

I want to give you some examples that may help you to dream up other ways you can infuse play in your marriage. When sharing a shower after the suds are washed off, drop down, and give him some love. Wake him up by licking and nibbling his morning erection. Wear your thong just a above your tight pants while climbing stairs in front of him. When you're out sitting together, drape a coat over your laps, cop a feel underneath it, and whisper how you'd like to do much more when you get home. Put on some saucy music and wear a revealing dress and heels and give him a sexy strip tease. Keep in your head your aim to surprise him every now and then. That goal will alert you to ideal moments for excitement. When the moment seems right, go for it.

Do not forget to build sexual tension beforehand. Building anticipation of an event sets it up to be memorable and enjoyable for both of you. Having already built up expectation alleviates any nervousness and moves past the sometimes challenging task of 'getting things going' in the moment.

Setting the Mood for His Pleasure

When you're wanting to provide him with a sensual feast, it is important to lay the groundwork. Just as you enjoy candles, soft music, and enticing smells to get you feeling romantic, so does he. If he doesn't enjoy it (consciously) it may be worthwhile to get *you* in the headspace to fully engage in the moment. Of course he probably doesn't have the list of required preparation (we discussed earlier) in order to be fully present in a sexual experience. But he may care more than you think.

Put "Give your hubby a wonderful blow job" on your calendar. Start his day right with making him fresh coffee and something he loves for breakfast. Let him know you're planning something extra special for dessert tonight and you'd appreciate him being prompt. Make sure to help him in whatever way possible get setup for a good day. Wrap a sexy thong in a note reading, "Mind if I wear just this tonight?" and place it in his work bag. (You might want to write on the outside "For your eyes only" to avoid his opening in public). Then text him shortly before he'd be leaving work to make sure his mind is primed for the evening's events. Your text could read, "Thinking of what I'm going to do to you when you get home. ;)" Okay, next item you should take care of is the children, pets, or other potential distractors. Whatever works for your life, just make sure you won't have to worry about being interrupted. Now, think about what your husband wants when he comes home. Does he like the house to be cleaned, a snack prepared, or something else that would make him smile as he comes in the door? See if you can get those items done, so he comes home relaxed and feeling positive. Decide whether you are going to eat dinner beforehand or head straight to 'dessert' and worry about dinner afterwards. Try to plan ahead, so that you feel comfortable and you both can fully enjoy the evening.

What Should I Wear?

This is a fun one. Keep in mind, you are wearing something for *his* pleasure. Though it is not for your comfort, I find that I feel more sexy and uninhibited when I enjoy what I am wearing. If you don't have any sexy lingerie that you like, make a trip to Marshalls, TJ Maxx, Target or even Walmart -- they have a fairly good selection. It's worth trying them on to make sure it is something you would wear. Don't be shy, try on the clothes before you buy them. Every woman should have a good collection of skimpy, sexy lingerie to entice her hubby. Find some things you enjoy that compliment your body type. What kinds of articles should you buy? By now, you may have a sense of what your husband enjoys about your body. He may really enjoy your cleavage. If so, select some kind of push up bra that brings out those assets. If he prefers your lower back, you may want to choose something that shows off your butt and thighs. Select something that is short enough to accentuate your legs and teasing him to see more. If you don't know, go with your preference. But, remember the name of the game is to wear something that is sensual and makes you feel like a fierce tigress, to make him feel like a king.

Now, back at home, you're in preparation mode. You may want to wear your make up a little heavy and wear some bright lipstick. This can give you a boost of confidence just by adding some extra. Put on your skimpy underwear and decide on a sexy outfit on top. You may want to leave your blouse unbuttoned an extra button or make sure your pants are especially tight, just to provide some intrigue from the start. Your husband is very visual and your outfit should stimulate him just by looking.

Your Quick Confidence Check

Don't let the enemy play with your mind. You are gorgeous and sexually desirable to your husband. Ask God to give you the right value on your body and ask Him to help you feel sexy and confident. I want to clue you in on something. I am not a supermodel. I still struggle in the areas of my weight. I am not skinnier than my husband. Even at my skinniest, I have weighed more. So, I am not your typical gorgeous wife asking you to do something I do not intimately understand. We, dearies, have to *choose* confidence. You have to choose that the pleasure of your husband is worth your confidence.

I remember many years ago reading an article in one of those cheap magazines that suggested if you feel bad about your body just turn out the lights or cover up with a sheet. I thought that was a good idea then. Now, I completely disagree. Tell Jesus about your discomfort and ask Him to show you how precious your body truly is. I came to a place of realization. There are really only two choices: a) either push through the discomfort, believe and present your body as *enough*, OR b) hide and let the romance of your marriage slowly dim and die. Believe your body is enough and do it *while* feeling afraid.

Steamy To Do:

Schedule a shopping trip this week and designate $50 to buying yourself attractive lingerie. Select the items that make you feel confident and accentuate the areas you know he would like.

Specifics of Amazing Peni

Step-By-Step Story

I'd like to firstly give you an overview of a possible scenario, then, I will break it down by stages of arousal, practical techniques, positions, and then troubleshoot some possible challenges. So, let's say your husband arrives home, and you are scantily-clad and everything else is taken care of. Now it's show time! First of all, in a seductive voice, you say "I'm glad you're home. I have a *great* surprise for you". You kiss his neck passionately and whisper "I think you're really going to like it". Then take his hand and lead him into the bedroom, sit him down on the bed, and help get comfortable. He probably will want to see the show, so propping him against the wall with a pillow would work nicely. Prop his back against the wall and position him with his legs apart so you can move in between. As you do, playfully say, "I've been waiting for this all day, baby. I'm so hot, I cannot wait."

Kissing his neck, you take off his shirt, then unzip his pants and pull them off. Kiss his chest and stomach; show your affection for this amazing man. You tell him how sexy you think he is. Use your hands to rub the areas you find most attractive. Tell him how you feel about those areas. Then, with his boxers still on, start to massage his upper legs and thighs with your hands. Begin to touch his shaft affectionately. Kiss around his package. Gently nibble and bite on his shaft. You enjoy noticing it becoming erect. Pull off his boxers, and get noticeably excited seeing his member for the first time. Say "Oh baby, I can't wait to suck on you". Look at it lovingly and kiss the shaft softly. Smile as you gently rub your fingertips along his shaft, gently pulling the skin up with your fingers.

Kiss all around his shaft with your lips. Use your tongue to lick from bottom to top the underside of his entire member. Get excited as you see his body tense with desire and pleasure as your tongue reaches his frenulum. Lick your lips to make sure they're especially wet, then move his member back and forth on your outstretched tongue. Take just his head into your mouth gently and leave it there for a couple of seconds. Take it out and smile, knowing that he can barely stand the teasing. You can see he wants you desperately to suck it all the way. Gently move your wet lips around his head and especially the ridge of his head. As he begs for you to go all the way, you feel yourself get more excited, and you tell him how much you love tasting his member.

Start with teasing motions of your mouth moving up and down his shaft with the entire penis in your mouth. First get to about ⅓ of the way down and then back up. Then go back to more random touching and teasing. Then do some circular motions with your tongue and lips around his penis. Then go down to about ¾ of the way and then back up a couple of times. Take his member out and wipe his wet penis back and forth on your face and cheeks--making sure to stimulate his frenulum in this process. Look into his eyes and say "Mmmm, this feel so good baby". Let the vibrations of your moans tingle on his member. Slowly, with wet lips, bring his member in your mouth and move all the way to the base of his penis for a deepthroat hold.

Then move in and out slowly. Feel the relief of his body, another involuntary response and his bodily gratitude that you finally made it to his especially happy place. From there, your upward and downward motions start to become rhythmic. But you interrupt the strokings with varied other sensations and teasings. You go all the way down and about ½ way back up and repeat, slowly at first but get faster as you continue. Take your mouth off and switch to a firm hand grasp on your husband's shaft. Holding it firmly and slowly, you move your hand up and down. As you switch between firm holds and faster sucks in and out, you continue to intersperse breaks for teasing and building tension. As you start to see him getting more excited and tense, you may notice his feet are curling and he's getting close to orgasm. Tell him you love seeing him turned on. Moan with pleasure as you see him enjoying more and more. Keep the pace and rhythm and increase. Use your forefinger and thumb to hold the base of his penis as you suck in and out more quickly.

Then, he gives the first involuntary orgasmic contraction and this cues you in that it is happening very soon. So, you increase pressure, moans, and speed until you hear that familiar heave as he releases the first ejaculation contraction into your mouth. You continue to suck but much slower in and out for each orgasmic contraction. Your tongue gives extra attention to the underside of his shaft. Keep moving until he has no more to offer and you gently provide one last suck from base to using your tongue to follow the undershaft to suck every last drop. You are careful around his head as it will be extremely sensitive right after ejaculation. (If he is uncircumcised make sure your last suck pulls the foreskin over his head completely to protect it. If he is uncircumcised you may want to avoid his head at the end because it will be very sensitive). But you end the experience with a gentle kiss at his glans and a smile. He looks at you with amazement and gratitude. "Honey that was incredible, you are incredible." To which you happily say, "It was *my* pleasure". Lay on his chest and let both of you enjoy the wonderful afterglow of the experience. Job well done, sister!

In that story, I went through a lot of the techniques that will be your bread and butter of oral. But I want to break it down a little more to ensure every area is understood and repeatable for you.

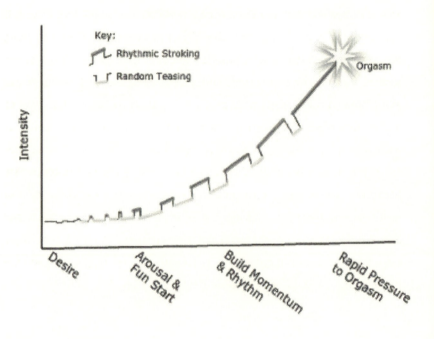

Stages of Oral Pleasure

Think about his stages of giving your husband head this way:

1) Desire

2) Arousal and Fun Start

3) Build Momentum & Rhythm

4) Rapid Pressure to Orgasm

As you move from one stage to the next, think of it as though you're leading him through each stage into and through his orgasm. Refer to Stages of Oral Pleasure visual included in your coursework.

Quickies are great, but a home-cooked, three-course meal is a gift to your marital intimacy. The time you spend in each stage varies considerably. Your husband may last anywhere from 2-3 minutes to 40 minutes or so [5]. If your husband is lower end or under of this range he may be experiencing Premature Ejaculation, which I provide some pointers in the Troubleshooting section. But for now, if that is his norm, try to dissipate the intensity as you move through the stages. Focus on switching it up so he won't become so excited to ejaculate before fully enjoying a full experience. If the time your husband lasts is on the longer end of the spectrum, the better you get at stages 1 and 2 and figuring out his particular pleasures, a "job" that previously may have been 45 minutes, could be cut in half or turn into just a handful of minutes. This timetable is also greatly affected by his level of focus and relaxation. If there are distractors happening during the act, it will take longer than if he were fully engaged. But, regardless of how long it lasts, you are *delighting* in it, and having fun pleasuring your beloved.

1) Desire

Much of my descriptions included in the last section can be considered part of the desire stage. I love a scene in the movie movie, *New York, I Love You*. At first it seems quite scandalous, but you may be surprised. The blonde actress walks outside a restaurant to smoke a cigarette. She forgot her lighter and motions to the man nearby on the phone. He nods and lights her cigarette. He hangs up and she comes closer to start a conversation. She talks about how she loves the city and being able to meet someone you feel you can talk to even a perfect stranger. "You know? When there's no past, no guilt. Have you ever made love to a perfect stranger?" He laughs uncomfortably, "Now you're teasing me". She replies, "I believe I am." Eventually she asks, "Am I bothering you?" He shakes his head, "Not at all". She says confidently, "You say that because now I've turned you on. Do you want to take me to bed?" He leans in to kiss her and she pulls away. She walks a few steps back to the restaurant entrance, "Who knows maybe we'll meet again" she opens the door and goes inside. If you're already cringing, the scene cuts to inside the busy restaurant. You find out the two "strangers" are married and sitting across from each other at the restaurant. Ladies, that is *desire*. After this incredibly steamy exchange outside, she whispers "I love you" and she begins to tear up as he grabs her hand and says "I love you too". The rest of their night is filled with laughter and vibrant indulgence with each other [6]. There was a sweet vulnerability about their second interaction that encapsulates the unique and beautiful dynamic of vulnerability and seduction within marriage.

Desire is a necessary stage in great oral sex. The most important sex organ is the brain. This is true for you and your husband. We have talked about being creative and getting your husband's desire flowing. As automatic as we think men's sexual desire is, he wants your seduction. He wants you to value this part of his desire. This is where the spicy lap dance, strip tease, sensual massage, skimpy outfits are important. On a personal note, it had been a while since I had done a particular kind of seduction that I know my hubby enjoys. But after I did it again more recently, he was very grateful. After the experience, he asked if I realized just how long it had been since the last time. I admitted I had no idea, so he then emphatically told me. It apparently was far too long ago. I laughed because I had no idea that firstly, he liked it *that* much and secondly, that he was keeping track of my choices of seduction. And thirdly, that he deeply enjoyed something that kind of made me feel silly (every time). I bet your husband feels the same way. He loves your seduction. Your husband's desire for sex does not begin in his pants, it starts with his mind.

2) Arousal and Fun Start

This stage is full of random touches and teasings, with minimal strokings and suckings, while your husband's member is filling with blood and it becomes elongated and hard. Your husband will enjoy some build up before you touch his member. Just as when your husband first touches your sensitive area--if there is enough anticipation--his initial touch can be an incredible feeling. First, play with his body. Grab his butt or his legs to pull him towards you to make him feel you want him. Tell him you want him. Spend time letting him enjoy various teasing techniques detailed below. All the while you're smiling and giving him desirous verbals. Begin to play with his member. This is an opportunity to let your husband enjoy the feelings of his penis becoming erect prior to rushing to the rhythm stage (though he may say that he'd like you to speed through to the next).

Here are some ideas. Give him unfocused and creative tickles, kisses, nuzzles, and nibbles (save the sucks and strokings for the next stage). Utilizing different textured surfaces--ie fingertips, palm of your hand, smooth side of your fingernails--pet his shaft to trigger the receptors in different ways and create unique sensations. Continue to talk to him throughout this stage with compliments and sexy seduction. Massage the base of the shaft. Lightly squeeze it with your fingertips. Using your forefinger, lightly pet all the way around the underside of the rim of his head. After a long wet lick around his member, hold it with your hand and do a soft sexy blow from base to tip, providing a cool sensation. Use both hands lightly grasping his wet shaft twist with each hand in separate directions. Very slowly take his head in your mouth, but just before your lips envelope the rim, stop and let his glans enjoy the wet warmth of your mouth as you use your hands to squeeze on his shaft. In this stage, be unpredictable, creative and explore new ways of using your fingers, tongue, lips, face, mouth and more. Flirt with sucking it all the way. Make him want it so badly. Enjoy, have fun, and let him know how much you delight in his "apple tree".

He may be unsure if he likes this stage at first. He will grow to trust you as he sees your understanding of his member, his likes, and the eventual pleasure you will bring him. The more you "build" during this teasing phase the bigger enjoyment he will receive in the grand finale. One last, but important note: keep in mind that you want to be moving from less sensitive areas to more sensitive areas. Consider how you would prefer your husband to give you a massage, then caresses all around your body, then moving delicately to your breasts, and eventually to your most sensitive crowned jewel. You would not wish him to go straight to your clitorous then move to a back massage. As you tease your husband, you should be moving from less to more and more sensory receptive areas. Keep in mind the anatomy lesson above. This stage is all about teasing, which means you are moving a little forward and a little backward then forward again in your journey toward rhythmic intensity (which is most pleasurable to bring him to orgasm). Be playful, have fun, and really delight in your husband's member.

3) Build Momentum & Rhythm

You will know to move to this stage when he has achieved a full erection, you are turned on, his body is starting to tense, and he is (verbally or physically) craving more. Remember, building tension and diffusing the tension and then building it again will make for better pleasure and a more powerful finish. This is the stage where the rhythmic strokings begin, using your mouth or hand. You want to slowly move into this rhythmic stimulation. Switch back and forth from the unpredictable, more random teasings of the previous stage and a couple of long rhythmic strokes and sucks. As you continue switching between, begin to move towards more rhythmic longer strokes and less of the random (review the chart to see how you're moving from more infrequent teasings to longer stretches of rhythmic strokings). You can also switch between long strokes down his entire shaft and shorter, more rapid strokes focusing more so on the head and upper shaft.

During this phase he should be fully wet with your saliva. As your husband will know intuitively because of his many years of practice, firmer strokes should generally be slower (He Comes Next). A less firm grasp should be faster. This means the sucks with your mouth should be faster. The firmer strokes with your hand on his shaft should be slower, generally. You can experiment with suction (your husband may love this or find it uncomfortable--you'll have to find out). At this point you can spend extra attention on the frenulum; lick it delicately while maintaining a tight grip on his shaft. You can maintain a grasp on the base of his penis with your forefinger and thumb while sucking in and out to give him a stronger hold.

4) Rapid Pressure to Orgasm

As you continue rhythmically up and down, if he says something feels good, keep doing that. You may notice an involuntary shiver, aka his first orgasmic contraction. This signals to you that orgasm is not far off. At that point, shift into final gear. Increase speed and pressure on his shaft. As you're sucking, lap your tongue against his very sensitive frenulum. Also increase your verbals, make excited sounds, words, and moanings. Show him that you're really into what he's feeling. At this point, your switches will just be from one rhythmic stroking to another, ie between hand and mouth, or particular variations of each. Realize any breaks, changes in your position, or distractions may decelerate your hubby.

You will be able to tell he's nearing orgasm, as his face and body will become more intense. Do not ask him if he's about to come as that or any question will detract from his focus. He may, however, offer the information. He may even give you instructions on what you can do to make this most pleasurable. If you're using your hand at this time put your mouth on his glans to ensure he receives the greatest amount of pleasure for orgasm. Then it will happen. When his first orgasmic contraction releases ejaculate, slow but continue your rhythm, and maintain pressure and full contact. Continue stimulating all the way through orgasm much more slowly. Maintain rhythmic motion and contact as he is contracting until there are no more contractions. Continuing pressure and movement during orgasm will ensure he has the most gratifying finish. Which is worth all of your loving effort. Give him some loving last licks and kisses and a warm smile as he relaxes in ecstasy. As he just came, be very gentle with the head of his penis. After orgasm it will be at heightened sensitivity and hurt-ability.

Techniques

If you've gotten this far, you've gotten a good amount of techniques incorporated already. But, I'd like to clarify. I need to remind you though, that the most important part of *any* technique is always your positive, generous, and "delighted" attitude. The virtuous wife in Song of Songs receives pleasure by pleasuring her husband. You are happy to give him a fantastic experience and his fruits are sweet to your taste. You want your husband to believe that is how you feel about it too. This is the *most* important part of any technique. I believe that is why we are only given this foundational clue in Song of Songs. If you adopt her loving and generous mindset about his member, you will have great success.

Teasing

Of course there are many things that can fall under this broad category. Teasing comes after seduction but some of the ideas below may be interchangeable amidst the two. My definition of teasing is any attention given to the penis, balls, or other erogenous zones that are not the full rhythmic stimulation building towards orgasm.

I'd like to give you some ideas:

-while seductively looking into his eyes, envelope your mouth around his finger (as though it was his member) and provide a long suck to his fingertip, then smile--include a moan if you'd really like to make him wild

-caress his inner thighs

-touch his member through his shorts

-massage the base of his penis

-tickle and caress his balls

-breath on and around his package

-kiss his balls

-tickle his balls

-press your fingertips into his shaft all the way around in different patterns

-nibble his shaft

-kiss in all different ways on different areas around the shaft

-lightly bite the shaft- this can provide an extra bit of excitement because teeth are dangerous in that area, but you can spice things up using them cautiously (*never* bite the head, balls, or rim)

-blow on the head

-kiss the head

-move his member around your lips as though applying lipstick

-kiss the frenulum

-lick the head like an ice cream cone

-use your fingertips to push the foreskin up from base to tip

-take very short breaks in between teasings to smile and get him anticipating the next sensation

Use your creativity to play with his package in all different ways. With your delighted and playful attitude, you'll be able to come up with many more ways to tease your honey.

Mouth Positioning

Your mouth should first of all wet his head and shaft when beginning any of the techniques, especially suckings and strokings. You have some options, depending on the fit of your mouth size and his member. Keep in mind you always want to avoid contact with your teeth. It can be incredibly painful for your teeth to catch his head. To avoid teeth, if your husband has a wider girth, you may need to cover your teeth with your lips (though not a sexy visual---it is the face people make when pretending to be a grandma without her dentures). Make sure your lips are sufficiently wet all the while. This can feel uncomfortable at first, but will get easier with practice. You may also be able to cover your bottom teeth with your tongue to avoid contact. If you have a little more space, you may not have to envelope your teeth, just be mindful to let your lips and tongue be the only things touching his member. Generally speaking, the tighter you can make your lips the better it feels to him. The tightness becomes especially helpful as you move into a more rhythmic in-and-out movement. If you are just getting started, do not feel compelled to try to put his member all the way in your mouth. Start slowly.

When feeling more confident after a couple of times (alongside practicing on your own), you may feel comfortable enough to try deepthroating which will come in handy in bringing him to orgasm. Deep throating just means taking his full member all the way into your mouth and throat. This is a very enjoyable feeling and visual to him. Check out the Troubleshooting section for more on conquering and working around your gag reflex. This is all very specific, but once trying it, you'll figure out what works for you and feels good to him. Just don't get worried about not knowing how to hold it in your mouth, go for it.

Up & Down Technique

This is the classic position that you will generally always come back to in Stage 3 and 4. Oral sex is meant to mimic vaginal intercourse to a large degree. This may help when thinking about the motions of your mouth in and out. Once you're ready to move to this motion, make sure your lips are sufficiently wet and move your lips over his head, taking him inside of your mouth, and slowly moving to the base of his penis. Make sure your teeth are safely tucked underneath your lips or tongue. Depending on your husband's preferences (or what you want to try at the time) you can move from the base all the way back to the tip or you can move back up to just before the ridge and then return to the base. You may want to start relatively slowly and begin to pick up the pace as you move into the final stages. During this technique, tighten your lips to increase the pressure (and pleasure) for him. You may allow your tongue to drag along the underside of his shaft as you move in and out. This stimulates the urethra (the path the semen will take from the testes) up to the frenulum. He will love as you take the extra effort to stimulate this part.

Suck Up Technique

This is a slight variation of the original Up & Down. Taking him into your mouth, move your head to the base of his penis. Then as you start to move back up, make your mouth hold him firmly and suck on him as if you were sucking through a straw. You may be able to feel the skin moving up some as your mouth moves back up to the head. Be careful to avoid contact with your teeth. Then return normally to the base and begin the suck up once more.

Swivel Technique

This is great to incorporate as you are continuing Up & Down. As you're moving him all the way in and out of your mouth, move your head back and forth as if swiveling. (Imagine an office swivel chair turning as the chair swivelling back and forth). This provides new sensations as you continue to build momentum.

Take a Quick Break

It may be an extra excitement for him if you stop all together for a couple of moments as you are beginning Stage 3: Build Momentum & Rhythm. This slows down the tension you're building, but can mean a more powerful orgasm by the end. Use the break to kiss his lips, push your breasts together and move your husband's member between them, or turn and give him a short lap dance. Then go back to the rhythmic stroking/sucking. As you go back down, notice the intense release of his body welcoming your warm, wet embrace again. This option has the potential to slow down his fast-tracked orgasm, but will increase the pleasure (and later mental memories) of his eventual finish. This will be at least mildly frustrating for him at first because it will stop the momentum you've been building with your rapid strokes to his orgasm. You should consider this in the teasing category. It can build anticipation to feel your stroking/sucking again.

Teeth Techniques

You may want to give him some thrill using your pearly whites. While holding his member, from the side bite his shaft gently. Of course though the shaft is less sensitive, you still want to take care not to bite too hard. While his member is in your mouth about halfway down, stop your movements and slowly bite--gently--on his shaft for a second. This will really get his attention, because it adds a jolt of danger to the experience which can be very exciting. This can get extra steamy if you give him a sexy gaze and teasing smile as you do this. You may enjoy feeling his member move or get harder involuntarily as a result. Then replace your lips, tucking your teeth safely away, and continue your motion. Do not use teeth on his head, rim, frenulum, or balls as they are way too sensitive. For these you'll want to basically hide your teeth behind your lips or tongue.

Licking Techniques

With just a little creativity, your tongue is a powerhouse of pleasure. Here are some ideas to get you started. Add to these through your own exploration and discovery with your husband and his preferences. These can be incorporated in Phase 2: Arousal and Fun Start phase or during the main event to switch things up.

-While holding (or stroking) his shaft with your hand, lick all the way around the head like a twister.

-With his member out of your mouth, lick up and down his penis.

-As you are holding his member, give him some strong, long licks on his head across the opening. -With his entire penis in your mouth, use your tongue to swirl your tongue one side and then then the other around his member.

-I would caution against licking or lapping very rapidly like a puppy dog. That is generally a turn off.

-Use your tongue to encircle and outline the rim (the area connecting to the shaft).

Lips and Face Techniques

Your lips have fantastic sensations to lend to the experience.

Ensuring your lips are sufficiently wet...

-Move your lips around his shaft up and down, while his penis is outside of your mouth.

-Give him kisses and nibbles with just your lips anywhere and everywhere.

-Nibble the underside of the shaft, without teeth.

-Push his member around your lips and move it with your hands onto your cheeks and across your face. Use your lips to stimulate his frenulum as you slide him all around.

He will also enjoy seeing his member on your face, this will probably be an incredible turn on for your husband. It shows you are clearly comfortable around his member, you enjoy being there and it makes him feel intimately connected with you.

Side to Side Technique

Holding his member in your hands, extend your tongue out of your mouth. Place his member on either side of your tongue. Move his member from one side of your very wet tongue to the other. Give him adoring looks as you stimulate his ever sensitive frenulum. You can also follow his penis with your tongue on either side licking all the while. This is an amazing teasing technique to intersperse into the later stages of arousal to help build his anticipation. It is very pleasurable because you are providing unique contact with the frenulum and you are showing your husband how much you enjoy the experience with your playful and fun expressions.

Tickle His Fruits

The balls are very sensitive to the touch. Many men enjoy their soft and gentle stimulation using your thumb or fingers. Ensure that you are handling with care, do not squeeze, bite, or pinch them. Light touching and fondling with your fingertips can be very pleasurable as you are sucking on his member. Licking and sucking on them can also be pleasurable for him, as you're taking a short break from specific attention on his member. Insert an activity like this around Phase 2: Arousal and Fun Start. Lick them slowly in circles. Not all men enjoy having attention on the balls, so it may be something you'll need to try out caringly and ask him about.

Driving Stick Technique

In this technique you are primarily using your hand. You want your hand to essentially mimic the in-and-out motion of the penis and vagina. Your husband will be very familiar with how he likes this to be done. Make sure you have his penis sufficiently wetted prior to using your hand. Feel free to use your mouth to get everything wet. A dry rub can be pretty uncomfortable, if not painful. When you move up, your forefinger and thumb should overlap his rim to provide for stimulation to his head as you stroke. As you are getting the hang of this technique, I would strongly encourage you to ask your husband to show you how to do this. He can model it for you, then you can try. Ask him to put his hand on top of yours and show you exactly how he likes it.

If you are nervous that he can bring himself to orgasm using his hand much better than you, let me ease your mind. Dr. Kerner says, "Men produce significantly higher levels of testosterone when they are being touched by someone else as opposed to themselves" [7]. Your hands, though less practiced, are going to feel better than his hands on his own body. Keep at it, and keep asking him to show you how he likes it.

On his shaft, you will be surprised at how much pressure it can handle. Ensuring he is sufficiently wet, grasp him with a hard hold. Your husband will let you know if your grasp is too tight (but I don't think you'll get close to that). As you are stroking with higher pressure hold, you don't need to go as quick. A looser hold can be quicker. At times, you can put your mouth on his head while stroking to give more sensation.

No Hands Technique

Your husband may really enjoy the unique sensations that accompany this technique. Without using your hands to hold his member, you'll have to employ some different pressures with your mouth for balance, those are very pleasurable and unique sensations to him. Though it may not feel very different to you, use this to switch things up a bit. To do this, while he is standing or sitting on the couch or bed, put your hands behind your back and do some of the techniques mentioned.

Hubby Thrusting Technique

Your husband probably likes the idea of thrusting into your mouth. He will be moving himself in and out of your mouth while you remain stationary. Unless you already have a good system worked out, this will be something you'll want to talk about beforehand. The easiest, and probably most comfortable for you, would be for you to kneel in front of him lined up with his member while he is standing. He'll probably want to hold your head with his hands while he thrusts in and out.

Already mastering deepthroating will be necessary for this technique. If you haven't yet but would like to try this, you can somewhat control his movements if you hold the base of his penis with your hand while he thrusts. A firm grasp there, may even increase his enjoyment. Keep in mind during this technique/position, you'll want to keep giving him positive facial expressions and show that you enjoy giving him this pleasure. Determine when it's enough and signal him to move back and give control back to you. To end this technique, give him a couple of generous sucks to remind him that you are enjoying yourself too.

During this technique some men can get carried away, and move too forcefully. The position is such a pleasurable visual for him and puts him back in charge (which he is probably used to). I'd encourage you to be proactive during the act if his movements make you physically uncomfortable. Simply take a firmer grasp of the base of his penis and stop his movements before it gets too fast or difficult for you. If it is just too uncomfortable, move on to something else. If it really got out of hand, make a mental not to talk about this later---it is usually not a great time to talk about it in the moment. Do assert yourself when necessary, but a preemptive conversation about this technique can go a long way to ensuring it is a positive experience for both of you.

Exhilarating Experiments

During the Stage 2: Arousal and Fun Start, why not experiment with some more unusual sensations. For a chilling and refreshing sensation, try bringing some iced water in the bedroom and get your hand cold and wet to surprise your honey with a refreshing sensation. For the adventurous, try incorporating melting ice cubes. I would talk him through this one, and make sure he's ok with it as it can be quite a shock. You can hold the ice in your mouth while sucking on him or use your hands to incorporate it (the latter may be too cold, see what he likes).

Bring in some tasty delights like whip cream or chocolate sauce and spread it on your honey's member. Enjoy licking off the sweet sauce as you're getting started with the experience. You could also use fresh fruit. While he is lying down, after putting them on around his member, you can seductively eat them off. Engage all the senses when enjoying the experience. It switches things up and makes it more exciting and fun for both of you.

Most Important Technique Of All

As you are practicing and growing in your sexual confidence, I want to let you in on a key secret. The truly confident wife is happy to ask for and receive advice. As history suggests, this is the mark of a true champion. When someone is able to acknowledge what he or she does not know and seeks the person who does for teaching, they are on a narrow road to mastery. So, recognize that it is actually confidence that allows you to approach your husband humbly to ask for his guidance. As you have established some good positivity and communication about sex, with your enthusiastic attitude, I am confident he will be more than happy to show you whatever you want to know about giving him amazing oral.

Ask him in a sexy and confident way to tell you exactly how he'd like you to hold him. Ask him if he likes how you're sucking it. Ask him to show you how hard to grip. Ask questions like: "is this the way you'd like my hands?", "is that too tight?" or "is that strong enough?" During the act, asking many questions will probably distract him, so ask a couple of questions and take a couple of risks. Often you'll be able to tell if something you tried was a real winner; he may say it in the moment. Or ask him what he thought afterwards. After the final event, ask him what parts he most enjoyed. When receiving his feedback, don't take anything personally. Instead be super curious about what he likes. The more you do it the better you will get.

Remember to check your attitude. Are you enjoying the intimate exchange with the love of your life? Don't forget your purpose is to give him a loving, enjoyable experience. He is not a machine but a human to be discovered and enjoyed every time you go down on him. Stay engaged with him. Remember this is not a performance but a connection that is building intimacy with your lover. And *delight* in delighting your husband.

Write in your Workbook #47. Jot down the techniques that most resonated with you. When can you incorporate your new knowledge? As you're getting comfortable, I would encourage you to make up a routine. Variation is one key to a masterful experience. Write 2-3 techniques in each stage that you'd like to do with your hubby next. (Feel free to take the banana and practice them in the bathroom first. See next section). Review each section, so you can feel confident to try out the new ideas.

Steamy To Do:

Practice. That's right, it's time to go for it. You won't ever get better without hands on practice (literally). Thankfully your practice will be both enjoyable for you and your husband. Remember your delighted attitude and go for it!

Positions for Amazing Visuals

Position Guidelines

I have included this section because having some ideas or guidelines makes women feel more comfortable to get started right away. There are a couple of things to remember in terms of positioning that will make it most enjoyable for your man. There are a couple of caveats to each of these guidelines, but for the most part, your position is wonderful if it includes these four criteria.

1) He gets to see your body (especially his favorite parts--do you know what these are yet? If not, ask him!).

2) He gets to see your mouth connecting with his member.

3) He is comfortable.

4) You are comfortable.

Do not feel like you have to stay in one position throughout the entire event. It may be extra pleasurable for him to receive varied views of your body while you're giving him pleasure. However, I would advise against switching positions when you're nearing the end of Stage 3: Build Momentum & Rhythm going into Stage 4: Rapid Pressure to Orgasm (unless you want to slow his movement to orgasm--in which case, switch it up!) Feel free to incorporate variations of each of these positions for your comfort and his pleasure.

Sitting Pretty

This is the first position I described in the story above. In this position, your husband is sitting on the bed with his back against the wall or headboard. Prop a pillow behind his back and neck so he can fully relax. You are positioned between his spread legs.

Variations:

Crouching- You can be crouched sitting on your knees with your elbows and arms in front, ready for action.

Cobra- You can be laying in between his legs with your elbows propping your chest up (like the yoga pose: cobra) to give you plenty of mobility.

Cat Pose- Probably the most appealing view for him in this position would be the cat pose. You are on your elbows and knees. You can use your elbows to support and free up your arms and hands. If you choose the cat pose, I'd encourage you to feel frisky during the act and arch your back down and pushing up your bottom to give him a full and wonderful view. At the same time, your cleavage will be seductively spilling over your bra (or lack thereof) which will provide another pleasure shot for him.

Your husband would love to see your full body, so switch up your angle so he can see more of you. If you pivot your body all the way to the right or left (so your body is perpendicular to his legs) this is great to see the entire profile of your body. He probably would even enjoy running his hand up and down your backside while you're giving him pleasure. Sitting Pretty is also a great position for you if you are pregnant, as the cat pose leaves plenty of room for a baby-belly. Another good option early in pregnancy is propping a couple of pillows up under your chest and laying on them while in any variant of this position.

Sitting Pretty v2

This is fairly similar to the first, but it allows you a couple more options. The major difference would be sitting him in a chair or couch. This way, you can be kneeling in front of him on the floor. Put a pillow under your knees to alleviate any discomfort for you. You can simply kneel on the pillow close enough to his package that your hands can hold onto the chair for your balance (holding onto his legs for support may distract him).

Variations:

Cat Pose- You can choose the cat pose here, which again provides those extra exciting views for him.

Standing- To give another exciting view, you can stand with your legs a little more than shoulder-width apart and bend at the waste. This is exciting for him to be able to see your whole backside and imagine what you look like from behind. If your lingerie is still on, he may enjoy glimpsing this as you move your head up and down.

Pivot- You can also pivot your body to the side as the show continues to give a profile view of your assets.

Outstanding Pleasure

You may have guessed your hubby will be standing for this one. For his comfort you will want him to be against a wall or leaning on something to stabilize him. Make sure it is sturdy--you wouldn't want the thing he's leaning on to break or both of you toppling over during the event (also if he's concerned about this it could be quite a distraction). This could be a fun position for surprise experiences. Maybe you spring this on him in the kitchen or in the bathroom. You can be standing and bend at the waist to give him a fuller view. Or bring a pillow under your knees to kneel.

Sixty-Nine

If this is new to you, I'll give a quick explanation. "69" is considered a mutual pleasure pose. Look at the number 9. Now use your imagination to think of your husband's head is the circle on top and his genitals are the bottom end. Then imagine you are the 6 with your head at the bottom and your genitals are the top end. If this is something you're not immediately comfortable with, join the club. Unbeknownst to men, it is an incredibly vulnerable position for us. So, if this is something you or he are interested in trying (or he is), you may want to ease into it. If you are not a fan, realize your husband may really be turned on by the experience. Keep in mind, he loves tasting and looking at you, up close and personal. You will probably feel more comfortable having had a shower beforehand and a recent shave. But, rest easy knowing he *loves* how it looks, tastes, and feels to be in and around your intimate area. Just as you cherish and love all things about his as well. This position can be most comfortably accomplished on the bed.

I'd suggest this as a more of an excitement-building pose. It is something that can increase excitement for him, but probably not a position in which he'd be able to orgasm. Trying to focus on both his pleasure and pleasuring yours makes it difficult for him to really enjoy, moving towards orgasm. It can support the experience, but don't use this when thinking about the endgame. Continue this position for a while and then switch to something where he can focus solely on the pleasure he is receiving to move to climax.

Bed Show

In this position, you are lying on the bed and your hubby is standing beside it. This can be helpful if you are not physically comfortable on your knees in front of him. Depending on the height of the bed, you may need to be in cat pose while in this position or you can prop yourself up with some pillows.

Variations:

Pivot- You can pivot to the side to give him more opportunities to touch and see you.

On Your Back- Another more adventurous option is lying on your back with your head hanging off of the bed. This is not a great option for your own control, but your hubby may like it so he can thrust as described above. I would only allow this last variation if you've had some positive experience with thrusting already. If you're not sure he understands your limits or comfort level, it would be hard to slow him down in this position.

Bed Play

Another position that allows him to thrust and lessens your movement is Bed Play. While you're laying on the bed he would be kneeling and/or be bent over you. You may be able to lift your head some but he would generally be in control here. This position allows you to relax a bit (especially if you're getting a little tired) and lets him thrust in the way he enjoys. Feel free to switch when you want to take back control. As mentioned, this option also put him in control. You need to be sure he is careful not to thrust too fierce. Before attempting these you may need to have a discussion, especially if he has been too forceful in the past.

Variations:

Straddling- He could also straddle your neck and thrust from that position.

Sidelying- You could lay on your side, propping your head with some pillows. He sits or kneels beside you and he can thrust in and out. You may be able to take back some of the control in this variation.

Some Spicy Extras

I would encourage these ideas after you're feeling more comfortable. When you've had some pleasurable experience where you both have built mutual trust and understanding. At that point, you'll be at a level that you may want to spice things up a bit more.

Tie Him Up

Try loosely binding your husband so that he cannot use his hands. This may sound too kinky and bizarre to you, but let me tell you why it may be worthwhile. I'm not saying you need to break out handcuffs (though you could). You could even take a scarf and tie his hands loosely behind his back. The point of this is to give you all the power. Even if he wanted to help, hold your head, lend a hand, or thrust, he can't. *You* are in charge. Feel free to discuss the idea with him in advance as not to freak him out.

As I mentioned, because men are conditioned to take the lead in the bedroom this gives you all the control [8]. Solomon's wife instigates and is forward with her desires and pleasures. You should not be silent and limp in the bedroom. You may be surprised how much your husband can enjoy himself when you remove all pressure for him to perform.

Blind Folding

This is another option that relieves all performance anxiety. It may produce another form of anxiety (much more pleasurable), as he will have no clue what to expect when the blindfold is on. As long as you've built up a reservoir of trust and pleasure in this department, blindfolding can be incredibly enjoyable for him. Because your husband won't be able to see what your doing the additional level of suspense can be particularly exciting. He may expect you to do certain things, but you switch it up. You're welcome to move your body so he can touch you and visualize how you look. Or in the Sitting Pretty pose, you can lower your pelvis so he can feel your underwear (or lack thereof) on his legs. Keeping him guessing and enjoying the surprises will add immense excitement to the experience.

Change of Venue

Though the bedroom is often the best place to do any of these, giving him some pleasure outside of the usual gives an additional spark for both of you. You may want to rent a hotel room just for the night to have a particularly memorable evening. Or you don't need to go that far and spend any money. Have you "christened" every room in the house yet? You may be surprised at the extra fun it is to enjoy each other in the bathroom, shower, hallway or kitchen. How about your backyard or balcony? This could be a great way to steam things up under the stars or in your camping tent to ensure privacy. Different times of the day also adds flavor. Why not meet at home for lunch hour and have a "dessert" ready to serve him as he walks through the door. Or surprise him while brushing his teeth in the morning with an "oral routine" he will never forget. The more unique memories you can serve him the greater desire and mental imagery he'll have in the in between times. These greatly produce and increase desire for both of you (as you know which is *incredibly* important).

Practice Loving It

If all this 'loving his member' seems totally out of character for you, I'd encourage you to practice without him around. I do mean *practice*. If you want to get good at pleasing your man, it takes practice. Take a banana still in the peel. Wash it, then cut one end off and scrape off any of the ridges so it's pretty round. Keeping the peel on keeps it pretty sturdy, but the banana without some of the peel will get a little wet, which will help in your practice. Alternatively, use an ideally shaped cucumber (especially if your honey is wider girthed). Then take it into the bathroom. It'd be best to do this when no one is home so you can practice without fear of interruption.

In a really sexy voice, practice talking to the mirror about his wonderful member. Practice looking like you really want it. You cannot wait to enjoy his fruits and receive great delight by pleasuring him. If you're really struggling with what to say make up sexy answers to the following questions: What does it feel like? How does it make you feel? What kind of desirous sounds can you make while giving it teasing kisses? Breath heavily as you imagine him increasing in arousal. In the mirror, get really good at talking about this sexy, manly member. Imagine you're the wife in Song of Songs, who so boldly describes what she'd like to do to her husband and how much she delights in it. Practice saying the colorful language you want to start using in the bedroom. Your goal is to make him feel like a king. You *love* his member. As you develop a vocabulary of descriptors practicing by yourself, it will become so easy to whip those out in the bedroom.

Write in your Workbook #48. As you're practicing, what are the areas you feel most confident? What areas do you need to work on more? Glance back in your workbook to how you'd like your husband to act, feel, and say when he's kissing your flower. Now turn it around. What do you think *he* would want to hear from you? Jot them down.

Try out some of the new positions you've learned this week. And give him at least one surprise experience in an unexpected place. I am sure you both will really enjoy!

Removing Your Possible Barriers

Troubleshooting For You

I am so proud that you have made it this far in the course! I have asked you to stretch in ways that may have been uncomfortable and challenging. The fact that you have pushed through to the end is a sign of movement toward mastery. Of course we each have our own story and may have hang ups on certain areas that have not yet been addressed. Below, I am going to cover some common issues that wives face when giving head, including: 1) Getting Tired; 2) Gag Reflex; 3) Grossed Out by Cum; 4) Deep Throat Difficulties

1) Getting Tired

This is a common concern. If you feel like he's taking too long to reach orgasm, there could be a lot of reasons behind that. Firstly, some women would envy your good fortune because that probably means he is on the longer end of the timing spectrum discussed earlier. But your sisters' husbands who are on the shorter end have it a lot easier when it comes to oral sex. Do not be dismayed, there are many ways to handle this (pun intended).

Don'ts - Let me first tell you what *not* to do:

1-   Do not tell him you're getting tired. If you do, he may ask you to stop right then and there (though he really wants you to keep going. It just feels that good!). At the least, he'd be distracted and feel pressure to orgasm quickly--which will derail or at least slow down his progress. It will also make your next attempt much harder because that will be in the back of your and his mind.

2-   Do not give a tired look or negative facial expression. That would also hinder his focus. During the act, he's still your kind, loving husband who doesn't want you to feel uncomfortable or tired, especially just for his enjoyment. You *want* him to relax and relish the experience. You do not want him to feel like you're doing him a favor or accomplishing a chore.

3-   Do not let on that you are not having a good time. You may have to strengthen your actress abilities. Try the suggestions below as though you were just wanting to tease him in a new way (though you will also be alleviating the discomfort for yourself).

4-   Do not start worrying that he's taking too long and you did something wrong. These worries will inhibit you from fully engaging and it will show on your face. Remain positive and excited. There are a million reasons it could be taking extra long, but there are plenty of good solutions outlined below.

Solutions:

1- Firstly, some of the issue may be ensuring your husband is sufficiently excited and seduced, in Stage One: Desire, before even beginning to touch his member. That expectancy before the event helps him to put his mind solely on the now. Just as with women, the less mind distractions the easier men orgasm. This is another good reason to set the mood and make sure he is comfortable. Once you have begun giving attention to his area, you can spend additional time teasing him, so he gets very hard in eagerness. This will allow his desire to be very heightened when you finally take him into your mouth. This may help him orgasm sooner.

Breaking up the strokings with teasing not only makes his orgasm more intense as mentioned, it is also a welcome break for you. Though, you shouldn't let your face reveal you're feeling tired; that will distract him. Try to break it up with teasings earlier on, so that when he's building to orgasm, you're fully rested to go with him all the way to orgasm. Also, fully enjoy the teasings. Be creative and have fun. It's fun to make the love of your life wild with desire. When you're enjoying yourself, he'll enjoy himself more too.

2- As you get more used to peni, you will build greater stamina and be able to handle longer stretches of the in and out movements. Just as you use an unfamiliar muscle for the first time in a while, it easily becomes sore. But, once used consistently, the muscle no longer gets sore or inhibits your performance.

3- Get in a more comfortable position. Maybe moving to the side or into another position that is more visually generous to him will be a benefit for both of you.

4-   Breaking the movements up by switching to use your hand allows your mouth and jaw to rest while continuing momentum. Or switch to using both your hands and your mouth in tandem. You could stroke with your hand and rest your mouth on just the head, moving your mouth when hand is moving up or over the head.

5-   If in either Sitting Pretty position or another bed position, experiment with bouncing the bed using your hands while his member is in your mouth. The bouncing pushes his body rhythmically into your mouth. This can help you to not expend so much effort (though it could be distracting for him, you'll have to do trial and error on this one). If you are kneeling in front of him, your hands can grasp his pelvis and pull him in and out to take care of some of the laborious head and neck thrusting movement. If doing Sitting Pretty v2, you can hold onto the couch or chair to help you pull in and out.

6-   Often you can speed him up to orgasm by being more aggressive and holding him harder/firmer and faster. Use lots of moans and enticing language that lets him know you're happy and loving his enjoyment. Remember to use that initial pre-ejaculation orgasmic contraction to begin being more aggressive to quickly escort him to orgasm.

7-   Switch to the Hubby Thrusting technique (best if he is standing and you're on your knees) so you don't have to do all the motion yourself. You wouldn't have as much control this way, but when getting tired it may help you to rest somewhat, and you won't interrupt his progress to orgasm; in fact he'll *love* this. (Remember not to tell him that's why you want to switch to this position!)

If you are doing peni on him in the shower or another place where you necessarily will be in an uncomfortable position for the duration, letting him have a little more control with the Hubby Thrusting technique will also provide some relief for you.

8-   While in the Sitting Pretty position, ask your husband to hold your head (again fairly gently) and push it in and out the way he would like it to feel. This can be uncomfortable if too rough, so you may need to place your hand on his body to give him a signal to slow down or stop. He may really enjoy this and it gives you somewhat of a rest.

9-   You can always ask your husband to help you using his own hands. Ask him in a positive, confident, and playful way (not a defeated and disappointed way). Do plenty of moans, compliments of his member, kiss his legs and balls while he is using his hands. Stay fully engaged. Also, he may like you having just the tip of his penis in your mouth while he uses his hands. This will allow you to rest but he can still enjoy the feelings and visuals of your mouth and face. When you feel rested you can resume.

Make him feel you can't wait to touch and lick it again. If you feel like you need him to use his hands until he orgasms, put your mouth near the head, and stay fully engaged until he does. Hopefully he will tell you and you can resume with sucks as he enjoys a powerful finish. You're welcome to do this as you are starting to really understand his body, arousal stages, and his member. Eventually, you'll get to a level of confidence that your hands are better than his. Don't doubt yourself, you'll get there!

10-   If you feel too tired to continue, you're probably not giving him enough energy or excitement for him to get into it either. It may be best to switch activities. Peni is always a nice intro to intercourse. Let his already aroused member work for both of your enjoyment. He loves feeling that you want him, so be sure to ask him to come inside of you in an enthusiastic way.

11-   I'd just like to give you a gentle reminder, dear sister. Intimacy is vulnerable. Regardless of how good you get at practicing and how confident you feel in your techniques, this is still intimacy we're talking about. Sex in all its forms cannot be dumbed down to a simple formula. It is new and different every time. These solutions can help you build a foundational understanding and give you confidence to go for things you may otherwise not. But at the end of the day, you may make mistakes, act silly, feel embarrassed, make him uncomfortable, feel inadequate, start crying etc. I have experienced all of these. The good news? This is your husband! He is supposed to see you and know you in every area. No need to despair. Laugh at yourself and keep going. Or cry some and let him love on you for a while and try again another day. It's ok. You're ok. Every type of intimate exchange is moving your marriage closer together, and that is success.

2) Gag Reflex (aka the pharyngeal reflex)

This can depend on your husband's size and also your own natural reflexes. Your natural gag reflex probably developed from your childhood to avoid a very legitimate danger: choking. It served its purpose well. You safely made it all the way to adulthood. Thanks, reflex! But it is time to grow out of that now. How do you do this?

Firstly, be easy on yourself. Do not let the pressure of having to open wide worry you. Take it slow. Do what you are currently able to do. The most sensitive area on the penis is the head and frenulum, which should not be too much of a stretch for even the most sensitive reflexes. You can still bring him to orgasm by using your hand and mouth together. Any of the techniques described can be modified in this way: hold his shaft with your hand and use your mouth on his head to compliment the strokes. There are rare cases where his member is truly too large, and in that situation letting your hand augment your mouth will work great.

In cases that are actually about your reflex, I am confident you can do it. It is very pleasurable for your hubby if you take the full penis into your mouth. Let yourself take baby steps. Do what currently feels comfortable, so you can begin to enjoy and let your honey enjoy the oral experience. Do not feel discouraged. I believe you will be able to do this.

Practice. Yep take out the banana, plantain, or cucumber of choice and spend time practicing. If these items are too large, start out with your own tooth brush. Start by making yourself, your mouth, and your throat very relaxed. Open your mouth big in the shape you make when saying the letter "O" and simultaneously let your tongue out as far as possible. You'll be able to feel the back of your throat opening. Try experimenting to the edge of what you know your reflex can currently handle with the banana. Then, slowly but consistently push the limits of your gag reflex.

Make it a regimen. Before brushing your teeth every night, spend time in the bathroom going a little further. (Go ahead and lock the door to avoid some awkward conversations). Your tongue is a muscle and as it gets used to this in practice it will remember during the act. The point is that you completely relax the muscle. For some women, it helps if they flatten their tongue to the floor of their mouth and fully relax the throat. Exhaling before going deep in the mouth may also give more room. If you take a big breath before, it may create a force pushing your husband's member out. Keep at it. Your body will adapt and allow you to open your mouth and throat. No, this is not going to feel good in the beginning. It will be a process. Commit to conquering the process. Eventually, you'll get to a place where it is easy and even enjoyable.

A note that he may need help understanding: forcing it won't help. It may make you less likely to try again. If you think he will force you, have a conversation with him about this. Let him know you wish not to feel pressured and you'll do what you are able to do and eventually, if you can, you'll be able to do the whole thing. Keep motivating yourself. Remember how far you've come. It's not something that can happen overnight. This reflex at one time saved your life. Now you have to intentionally retrain it to be relaxed during what used to mean mortal danger. Also realize that your jaw muscles need to be stretched and will get stronger to allow you to open up all of the way. Be patient, you'll get it with consistent effort.

3) Not Fond of Ejaculate

I have certainly heard many women queasy at the mention of this part of oral sex. They see it as gross. They also wonder, "why would my husband even want me to taste his cum"?

Men hit a point in their journey to orgasm where they will ejaculate basically no matter what. Your husband may tell you he's coming, and you can see it happen a matter of seconds later. By that point, you could stop stroking entirely, even run out of the room, and he will more than likely still ejaculate. Women are not this way, we do not orgasm if things change at the last moment. A different stroke or sensation even a few seconds before we were about to orgasm can totally throw us off track [9]. So, if a woman can get all the way to orgasm, it's generally always a wonderful experience. But, a man can orgasm even if the last moments are incredibly disappointing because he already hit that point of no return. He will orgasm but it is not as powerful as it could have been.

The truth is, the sensation your husband feels when orgasming is so much stronger if stimulation and stroking is maintained all the way through every last orgasmic contraction til there is no more contractions or ejaculate. Even though he could still orgasm if you ignored his penis in those final moments, the best finish for him is if you show him your deep love and lead him through every last ounce of his ecstasy. If women realized that was the reason he really wants you to keep it in your mouth, I think they'd be more interested in obliging. All of her wonderful work has brought him to this marvelous point. She has the choice to keep his member in her mouth and end with his incredible moment in total bliss. Or she can cut short the experience and end it in disappointment.

Here are some solutions to the two major reasons women do not like their husband to ejaculate in their mouths: the taste and thought of it.

Taste -

Firstly, it is completely natural and harmless. Ejaculate tastes fine and it's very good for your marriage. You eat spinach because it's good for you, not because it tastes like ice cream, right? Swallowing semen is worth it.

If the taste is truly repugnant,

1- You can encourage him to lessen coffee, alcohol, and smoking to improve the taste.

2- He can also eat more fruits, especially pineapple, for a sweeter taste.

3- When he is ejaculating, slowly suck his member deep in your mouth. This way, the cum goes directly down your throat and you cannot taste a thing. He also will probably really enjoy that.

If you do swallow his ejaculate, you will get used to it. You may even begin to crave the taste. I had heard of this happening but only since experiencing the craving in the heights of passion, did I believe it truly can happen.

Thought-

Go back to imagining your husband going down on you. Most women do not ejaculate externally (some do), but let's pretend you did. Imagine you're getting close to orgasm and right before you explode with pleasure, your husband pulls away in disgust watching you ejaculate. That would *not* make you feel good. What if instead he drank of your sensual fluids and smiled as you enjoyed the immense pleasure of orgasm and afterglow. That would be a perfect ending. Realize that your husband is at the moment of ecstasy when he is ejaculating, what do you want on his mind? a) "Oh WOW!" or b) "Oh I hope I didn't get any on her, I know she hates it…" You could seriously arrest his focus and lessen his orgasm b)'s thoughts. I find it more important for my husband to enjoy this moment than me to make sure I don't taste the stuff. Whatever concerns that are coming up for you about it, push through them and realize your husband's experience and being loved well by you is worth it.

Other solutions-

If I haven't convinced you yet to just deal with the minor discomfort it can cause you (before you get used to it) then here's some alternatives. I am giving you alternatives only because if this is your only hang up and you won't go down on him if you have to swallow, then I need to give you some other options. (Until you get to a place where it is not mentally so hard for you to try and eventually enjoy). Make sure you have a candid conversation (way prior to the experience) if he wouldn't mind cumming somewhere other than your mouth. Let him know that you would like him to tell you when he is about to cum and you can take your mouth off and aim it elsewhere. No matter what you decide, keep your facial expressions positive and excited while he's cumming.

1- Have a napkin or washcloth nearby to catch it.

2- You can also ask him to cum on your body, breasts, or face. You may want to do this sometimes to switch things up (even if you normally swallow). Remember the visuals you give him in the bedroom go with him when he leaves, which supports desire for the next time.

3- A compromise: if you do not want to swallow, you can spit it out in the napkin (just do so discreetly).

My aim is not to keep you comfortable. I know that is not your aim either, otherwise you wouldn't be taking this course. I want to get you out of your "comfort" zone into "fantastic lover" zone. So, I do encourage you to work up to keeping it in your mouth, to allow him to stay focused on his pleasure. You're doing peni for *him*. Also, it is a lot more authentic to then nestle up to him and tell him how much you enjoyed it, if you didn't just stop the experience to pull out your napkin because his orgasm grosses you out. He would never want you to think he was dirty . Deciding to love his ejaculate is another step you can take to love and serve him well.

4) Having Trouble Loving His Member

If you're still having trouble getting to a place of true love for his member, I have addressed the general issues women have below.

Hygiene

I can understand if he is not clean, it is very difficult to bring yourself to do oral sex. But there are plenty of options that will solve this small issue.

1-   Encourage him to take a shower with you before the experience. If you do not think that is enough, you can even do the honors of cleaning his area. Do so in a playful and kind (and gentle) way. Be careful not to make him feel bad. During the event you can tell him how great it tastes. After you go down on him and he has a great orgasm, let him know how wonderful it was for you to suck on his clean member. I am pretty confident he'll get the subtle hint.

2-   As a second tactic, let him know you'd like to give him some surprises, but you're not sure if he'd be able to relax if he didn't feel clean. Ask him if he wouldn't mind coming to bed every night after taking a shower or at least using a washcloth on his area, just in case. He probably would be more than happy to include this into his nightly routine, considering the rewards.

3-   If the indirect routes are not working, using the Bedroom Talk Laws, bring up that you'd love to give him amazing head, but you're just a little concerned about the cleanliness. That gives him a lot of motivation to make it a priority.

Trimming

1-   This is also something you can bring up in a playful way. You wouldn't want to offend him about his package. He really wants you to love it and think of him as sexy. He may just be clueless that the pubes are getting in the way. Using Bedroom Talk Laws, ask him if he wouldn't mind trying to trim up down there. A male electric razor also works really well in this area.

2-   Feel free to adapt some of the cleaning suggestions for your trimming purposes as well.

Choice of Boxers/Underwear

1-   New and clean underwear are a lot more sexy than hole-ridden or stained ones. Buy him new ones and discreetly dispose of the others. Do not let something so silly come between you and giving your man amazing head.

Anything Else

1-   If there is another reason you're having trouble, see what creative ways you can brainstorm to fix it. If your indirect but kind approaches don't work, using the Bedroom Talk Laws (!!) and approach him about it. Remember, he wants you to love it. He is *very* sensitive about this, so please be careful and protect his ego. But do figure out what bothers you and get it corrected.

Write in your Workbook #49. Reference the Bedroom Talk Laws and draft how you exactly will approach him on the topic of concern. Be very careful and affirming. Decide beforehand in your journal what you will say and how you will say it.

2-   Spend time thanking God you have such a wonderful husband. Be grateful for his member (God's handiwork). What a simple and fun way you've been given to make him feel like a king. Be grateful it makes him fall madly in love with you all over again. All you have to do is will yourself to love it (at first) if you don't already. Count your blessings, dear sister, this is a great opportunity! What a wonderful, marital gift!

Write in your Workbook #50. List out all the things you're grateful for his member. Pray about it, ask God to help you to fully desire your husband. I'm serious. God put you two together "So they are no longer two, but one flesh. Therefore what God has joined together, let no one separate" (Matt 19:6). Get your head aligned with what God wants to work in your marriage.

Steamy ToDo:

Push yourself to go past your "comfort" zone and into "fantastic lover" zone this week. Put it on your calendar, prepare, and enjoy!

Helping Him Enjoy Peni

Troubleshooting For Him

1) Low Sex Drive

If this is true of your husband, you know all too well how painful a reality this is. Many wives wish their husbands would "have a headache" every once in a while, but there are many other women who can't understand why their husband is consistently turning them down. The pain and insecurity this causes in a wife is heart wrenching. If this is your story, I'm so sorry for the pain you have felt in this area. I hear you and want you to know, you're not alone. There are many reasons this may be happening. I want to go through many of the common problems and suggest solutions. As these solutions are focused mainly on your partner, make sure you approach him about a solution with grace, love, and prayer. This is a difficult reality for your husband too and you want your words and actions to move you both closer together, not pull you apart because you didn't think and pray through how to talk about something with him.

Do Not Deprive Each Other

The Bible is clear that husbands and wives should not withhold sex from each other. Your husband's body is not his own, it also belongsto you. I have seen husbands withhold sex from their wives as a power move. This may not be the case in your marriage, but getting a biblical understanding of the sex act is helpful. God made sure this passage was in the Bible to correct either husband or wife that may be withholding. In 1 Corinthians 7:3-5 it reads:

"3 Let the husband render to his wife the affection *due* her, and likewise also the wife to her husband.

4 The wife does not have authority over her own body, but the husband does. And likewise the husband does not have authority over his own body, but the wife does.

5 Do not deprive one another except with consent for a time, that you may give yourselves to fasting and prayer; and come together again so that Satan does not tempt you because of your lack of self-control."

It is important for you to realize that God's plan for your marriage is regular sex. He designed you to have very consistent and fulfilling intimacy in marriage. If your husband is not allowing this to happen, he is going against God's word. This is an area your husband needs to deal with before God and you can be a kind, loving, and generous wife who supports him. However, you cannot make him do anything and attempting to do so may undermine any progress.

Now that you know, it does not mean you need to shove this verse in his face and demand sex. Those "loving feelings" will run far away and your husband might follow suit. Instead, you should pray for him and pray for your marriage. Anyone outside of God's will feels that emptiness. Be patient, employ the solutions below, pray for wisdom, and carefully plan how to approach the topic (using the Bedroom Talk Laws). Write out what you want to say. The solutions below will give many suggestions of what he may be dealing with and what you can do to help.

Body-

In a world where we are constantly barraged by images of shirtless men with toned biceps and checkerboard abs, our husbands are very much affected too. He may not feel confident in his body and he doesn't want you to see him as less-than sexy. Instead of pushing through the discomfort (as I would advise him) he instead may be hiding. This is something that may be deep in his psyche.

Solutions:

1- You can support him by praying on your own so his self image improves.

2- You can also provide generous and consistent touch and compliments. You can come up behind him and kiss and tell him how sexy he is. Give lots and lots of encouragement in this area. Let him know that you *want* his body. You'll need to be consistent in your compliments because he will not trust you if they only come out every once in a while. If he is overweight, he more than likely has low testosterone as well low body image (check out that section below).

Stress-

Financial woes are one of the most common reasons for men to be too stressed for sex. Sometimes when we have money pressures in our lives we can feel helpless to know what to do or how to help. I shared briefly earlier that according to the following study, you may not need money to alleviate this pressure. "In one study, researchers at Dartmouth College and the University of Warwick, England, measured levels of happiness in 16,000 men and women...The researchers even found that sex is so closely tied to happiness that they estimated increasing sexual intercourse from once a month to once a week would have the same mood-boosting effects as adding $50,000 a year in income" [10]. So, what comes first, the chicken or the egg? More money or more sex?

There are many other reasons for stress in your husband's mind. Do you know what stressors are on your husband? If he is eternally frustrated at x are there solutions you can find to alleviate that pressure?

Solutions:

1- Try to alleviate the pressure of the stressors. Some of these are small changes that can be made immediately. Some may take time to fully work through, either way, prioritize getting past this inhibitor to your marriage. These are very important maintenance issues that need to be addressed in order to enjoy a fulfilling life-long marriage. You may be able to sign you both up for a Financial Peace (www.financialpeace.com) course meeting in your area and stick to a budget to get your family on the road to better finances, peace, and more sex. If he is stressed that the house is a mess when he gets home, can you prioritize your activities to ensure it is at least picked up before he walks through the door. If he is completely stressed by his commute, can you guys devise a plan to move closer to his work in the coming year? If he is the first person you run to about all of your problems and lean on him to solve them for you, maybe you need to take on a little more responsibility--go first to God and see if you can solve the issues before adding stress to your husband's plate. Can you be more prayerful about when to bring up concerns? I notice that if I bring up an issue (whether between us or something else I'm dealing with) while we're having our date time, it adds a negativity to the experience that wouldn't be there if I just held off.

2- Try scheduling regular date nights or rest days. Our church has given great wisdom in the area of rest. With their encouragement, D and I take a rest day weekly where we don't do or discuss anything stressful. We make sure we are having fun and relaxing together. This is also a great day to meditate, reorient, and are intentional about growing in our relationship with God. It is also very helpful for our marriage relationship. Amidst the many stressors of life, we take time to have a play day of sorts and it greatly increases our enjoyment of each other and our life together. Can you institute a rest day or date night in your household? Maybe just start with a day every week where you decide to be as stress free as possible and not bring up anything that will hinder that.

Write in your Workbook #51. If stress is an issue in your and your husband's life, make a list of each of the areas. Then write out possible solutions using some ideas above. Choose 2 to employ immediately. Make a plan of how to employ 2 more next week. Start slow, but do make sure you're lessening stress for the both of you. This is an investment in your future.

Depressed:

Another inhibitor to sex is depression. Your husband may be suffering from this mind difficulty. Is he unwilling to talk much? Is he avoiding friends? Does he not do things that used to make him happy? There are natural solutions listed below for low-level depression. If he is suffering from chronic depression he should be treated with professional support. For the health of your marriage, it is very worthwhile to invest in this help.

Solutions:

1- Pray for your husband and ask God to give him and you wisdom in how to address this issue. Ask God to heal him. Ask God to bring him godly relationships that can support him through this challenge. When someone is suffering from depression it is challenging to see past their own misery to what is happening around them.

2- If your husband is unmotivated to change, your husband may need to hear how his mood is making *you* feel. Using supportive and affirming language, bring this up to him. Support and love him and *gently* help him to see the need to work towards his own health.

3- Seek out alternative methods prior to considering medication, as medication can have many adverse side effects, including dampening effects on libido and even ability for erection. Exercise, energizing routines (check out the Miracle Morning book), meditation, healthy diet, and short-term therapy can give great relief and even cure low-level depression.

Medications:

Have you considered that his medication can be affecting his libido? Many medications have a powerful effect on sex drive. If he is taking antidepressants, anti anxiety, or antihypertensive pills (as well as other medications), they could be halting his natural libido.

Solutions:

1- Do an internet search and read all labels of his medications to find out if this is the issue. Continue your research to find out what are alternative or natural remedies to his condition. Something as simple as cashews have been known to have a mood-boosting effect on people suffering from depression.

2- These kinds of remedies are out there and worth your pursuit. What do you need to do to help him be healthy? Is there a more holistic doctor you can see who can treat symptoms more naturally without medications? Are there lifestyle choices that can help him reduce the medications? Do work on this. There is hope for his libido to return.

Low Testosterone:

Testosterone is a necessary chemical in your husband's body (and to a lesser degree in yours) that is responsible for a myriad of health benefits. It is significant in sexual desire, function and performance. Your husband's level of testosterone also affects "energy, bone mineral density, body composition, muscle mass, strength, mood, feelings of quality of life, cognitive function, as well improve particular diseases" [11]. Needless to say, it is important that your husband has sufficient levels of testosterone in his body to support all of these functions. To tell if he is having issues with low testosterone there are a handful of symptoms that may be associated:

- Low sex drive (libido)
- Erectile dysfunction
- Fatigue and poor energy level
- Difficulty concentrating
- Depression
- Irritability
- Low sense of well-being [12]

If anything mentioned above seems to indicate your hubby, it may be worth doing more research into low testosterone. Please do note that a doctor should diagnose low testosterone and medical testosterone supplement therapy should only be taken under the care of a physician as it can be very dangerous otherwise and even affect fertility [11]. The most common causes are a) not getting enough sleep, b) being overweight, and c) taking certain medications. The good news is there are very effective natural solutions which are very effective in boosting testosterone.

Solutions:

Working out - Firstly, working out increases serotonin, endorphins, and testosterone levels in your man. Each of these hormones positively affect his mood and testosterone affects the libido. Working out has a powerful effect on libido and every other part of your health, so devalue this vital help. Make working out a normal part of your marriage.

1- Surprise your hubby with a gym membership and a couple of sessions with a trainer. Maybe he'd be more motivated if you did something like this together.

2- Make a goal together to get in better health this coming month and commit to two gym dates a week. Usually when beginning to work out you need a jump start and serious accountability for the first couple of weeks. Once your body gets used to the pain of starting, you and he will begin to enjoy it and probably won't need external motivation to keep going.

3- You could talk him into signing up for a 5k in a couple of months, so you both can train for it. There are some pretty great apps to help in this, ie: Couch to 5k.

4- Does he enjoy a certain sport? Many men who normally wouldn't exercise can thrive in a competitive sporting environment. Do a little research to find some sports teams in your area that you could get him involved or maybe you both could do together (Meetup.com and Craigslist.com are excellent resources for finding these types of teams).

5- Try doing physical activities on your date night times to get him started. Working out is also a natural aphrodisiac. Just after he's hit the gym (or you went together), is a prime time for a roll in the hay. Why not invite him for a sexy shower together and see where it leads?

Food -

A healthy diet is vital to the health of his body and your sex life. Incorporating fruits and vegetables while cutting out the junk is an important first step. Alcohol and cigarettes (as well as other drugs) also need to be lessened or quit entirely as they inhibit libido. Be proactive about bringing healthy food into the house.

Lose Weight -

"Excess weight -- especially excess belly fat -- can affect sexual function in many ways; it can interfere with the body's ability to supply blood to the penis, for instance, and it can cause testosterone production to plummet" [13]. Helping him shed the belly will be key to getting him more consistently excited about bedroom activities. You could engage in Weight Watchers together or another accountability program to get him to take his excess weight seriously. Try out all of the work out ideas above. That will start him on the right track and the pounds will begin dropping off as he gets excited about his new workout routines.

Take Vitamins -

Ensure your husband is taking his daily multivitamin as it include vitamins vital for erectile health.

2) Trouble Climaxing

If your husband takes a long time to orgasm during oral or otherwise there are a couple of simple reasons and solutions.

As I have mentioned, most (if not all men) discover their penis in childhood. Any mother can tell you once the diaper comes off of her son, the baby touches and giggles. Little girls don't discover these sensitivities nearly as often. Your husband has a long history of understanding his member. Some men learn to masturbate with the focus on the most sensitive region, the head. This can have two possible negative results.

1) Because the act of intercourse or peni is very different than the way he has learned to orgasm for years, it may be difficult for him to achieve orgasm just through sex or oral.

2) It could have created the effect of premature ejaculation, due to learning to orgasm so quickly through masturbation.

3) Another reason for having trouble climaxing is that your husband maybe masturbating too frequently. Namely, if he masturbated earlier that day or even the day before, it could be harder to climax with you.

4) Another possible reason is he may be under the impression that a better lover lasts longer--informed generally by porn. Men sometimes think this is the only skill needed in the bedroom. Men (if developed this skill) have the ability to recognize how close they are to orgasm and slow things down to not

go over the edge. If he thinks you like the longer experiences, he may be intentionally be extending it.

5) Some men just take a long time to climax (your girlfriends may even be envious that your husband lasts so long).

Solutions:

As the average time of intercourse or oral before his orgasm is about eight minutes. You may be far over this time. Know that even 45 minutes is still considered normal (though that can be very tiring for the wife performing oral). If you are getting tired, there are lots of solutions given in the Troubleshooting section above. But one key I want to reiterate is the teasing. As you intersperse teasing in between your series of rhythmic strokes, that makes him more and more excited. Also, being very engaged with your words, body language, and facial expressions will give him more opportunities to relax and fully enjoy. Remember anything else on his mind distracts him from moving towards orgasm so try to make sure they are all gone. You can also focus a lot of attention on the very sensitive head, make your words and strokings more aggressive to speed things up as well.

The other possible reasons I mentioned obviously need to be talked through with your hubby, as he may be completely unaware of these possible reasons. I would caution that you be prayerful about when and how to bring it up. These topics can feel very personal and potentially embarrassing for him. I especially want you to consider the timing. If you are on a rocky place in your marriage where everything talked about the marriage bed is bringing up conflict, please wait. Wait until you both have built up some healthy confidence and enjoyment in this area. Then when you're sure he feels loved and appreciated, ask him gently about some of these things.

These issues are things you'll need to discuss with him, very carefully, honestly and tenderly. Review the Bedroom Talk Laws before drafting in your workbook what you will say. Write in your Workbook #52. Don't take a chance to talk to him without carefully planning. You can never take your words back, and they could really affect him. You don't want him thinking you're always getting tired and anxious for him to come while you're trying to give him pleasure (which would make it take longer anyway).

Masturbation -

If you both have never discussed solo masturbation in your marriage, it is something you need to determine between the two of you. If he or you have a much higher libido than the other, it can be a helpful augment to your marriage, especially in times of absence or travel. (It is not prohibited in the Bible). However, fantasizing or visualizing during must be faithful to the marriage covenant (Matt 5:28). If it becomes a habit it can be something that needs to be reigned in because ultimately your intimacy should be happening for both of you together.

As a couple you should explore your comfort level with this. I would encourage being very clear about what you would like and discovering what he would like in your marital intimacy. If he would not like you to do solo masturbation, then he also should abstain. If the solo experience is preferable to your husband, I would encourage you to tenderly and gently (maybe over time) understand the reasons why. As his wife, you want to be part of your husband's sexual fulfillment and he a part of yours. Having open dialogue about this activity is important between you both, as it can bring you both closer together or further apart. You may encourage him to engage in this with you as you can provide helpful enthusiasm, visuals, and the opportunity to grow closer together through this act.

I would also encourage mutual masterbation. This is just another way of lovemaking when there may be a physical reason to not engage in another way. It also may be an opportunity to vary lovemaking and yet still provide a supportive and loving experience. This is a helpful option if you are feeling too tired to do anything else. Watching him masturbate may also be visually stimulating for you. It is a great opportunity for you to learn more about his likes and pleasures. If he is struggling with insecurities, getting to a level of comfort where he can masterbate with you is a great sign. It may help him to ease into being more open with you in all of his sexuality. Try not to take a conversation or experience personally. If he would rather masterbate than make love to you there are some serious emotional reasons behind it. He needs to be encouraged kindly and not forced to share. Also, realize masturbating together is still intimacy and part of making love.

More Sensitive -

If your husband does not engage in masterbation for a couple of days, he will be much more sensitive and able to orgasm much more quickly with you. I would encourage much less masturbation to increase his sensitivity to you and your touch. I would also encourage you to become a master at oral (including using your hand), so the skill in your touch makes him orgasm more deeply and fully. Give yourself to this pursuit for a time. Once you've worked to master this skill, you'll be able to utilize it any time without as much effort as at first. Use this book as a guide and practice, practice, practice.

3) Early Ejaculation

This is the most common sexual dysfunction for men. This is such a deep insecurity for men because it threatens their manhood. They are under the impression to please their women they need to have a forever erection. Which is just not true. Many men avoid sex for this insecurity or they run to medications that can actually exacerbate the issue and cause dependence (which is great for the pharmaceutical companies). It can also cause a psychological dependence, worried that he can't please you or will disappoint you without this medicine. There are many things you can do to slow things down in the bedroom. You

Solutions:

1- Your husband can develop his skill in recognizing his level of stimulation and slowing down. He can employ the stop and start technique which will extend the time.

2- Switching up sex positions will allow space for calming down a bit while continuing the experience.

3- Practicing Kegels will also give him help in being able to control his ejaculation.

4- Learn to slow things down. Some men arrest their orgasm because they are trying to last longer. But once they hit that moment of "no return" trying to slow down just makes their orgasm less powerful. He and you need to become sensitive to his level of arousal and slow things down before he gets to that spot.

When he reaches that first orgasmic contraction (without ejaculating) he is very close to orgasm. At that point, you'll want to slow things down. Take a couple of minutes to kiss his thighs, chest, lips, and let him know how much you love him and find him so sexy. Begin massaging other areas of his body. You may want to tease him by touching yourself for his enjoyment (but remember you're focusing on him right now, so don't shift focus to your pleasure or it may be frustrating for him). Then go back to pleasing him.

5- Until you're wanting him to come, focus less attention on the head. You can also squeeze his head in a way that actually pushes the blood building up in the head back down. If he generally orgasms quickly, he may be able to teach you how he does this with his hand to allow him to slow down.

Your Fulfillment

If his inability to last for very long is affecting your fulfillment there are also some solutions. Be very careful bringing this up. This is tied very closely to his confidence and may really hurt him if not dealt with gently and carefully. If there is resentment towards him because of this problem, it may be rooted in your not feeling fulfilled. It is important for you to feel fulfilled sexually. Create a culture where your orgasm is the first thing both of you focus on in lovemaking so you are already satisfied by the time you are bringing him to orgasm. As you understand your own sexual response, you'll see he can stimulate you and bring you to orgasm (or you can using your fingers or a vibrator) without his being inside of you. Thus, his length of erection won't be an issue. Use the Bedroom Talk Laws in bringing this up to him. Be very encouraging. Most men are way more insecure about their member, its size and how long it lasts than you can ever imagine. Love his member, and love the way he arouses. Give him lots of loving and positive feedback to encourage him in this area.

4) Difficulty Erecting

Recognize every man will have difficulty erecting or staying erect every now and then. There are many factors that could contribute (some of the solutions listed above will be very helpful to do--especially those for Low Testosterone). A major cause of erection difficulties is anxiety. Especially if he has had difficulty erecting before, it makes him worried it will happen again. "Whenever a man has anxiety, his hormones send out signals to clamp down on his blood vessels, including those feeding the penis. If he's afraid he won't be able to get it up and keep it up he will create a self-fulfilling prophecy in which he physically can't, leaving him worried about sex (and having less sex), as well as feeling ashamed, angry and abandoned" [14]. Realize it has nothing to with your attractiveness to him. It can happen to any man at any time. Talk with him about this. Normalize this for him. Let him know you know that it is normal. Take the pressure off of him. Do not take it personally and let him know it's really no big deal and do other things you both enjoy intimately.

As the average man is having full or partial erections many times per day, he may be having more than you think. If he has a nightly erections, then you can be sure it is not a physical issue, but a psychological one. As I mentioned in the Understanding His Erections section, though there are multiple reasons for his erection, any erections can be used for sex. If stress or emotions are doing a number on his ability to become erect, try using his morning erections. In the morning he has higher testosterone levels and lower stress levels. He also may be less aware of insecurities that would normally inhibit him because he is still waking up. Wake up a little extra early, brush your teeth and get fresh. Why not then wake him up to your warm wet mouth around his member, giggling, and enjoying?

Heat Up Desire

Imagine your husband's desire is a wheel moving up a hill. You are the one that will need to give pushes. As you give one push it propels his desire a ways forward but then he'll need another one. But as you continue to give pushes, you build inertia and the wheel will begin to move on its own. You may have to spend the next couple of weeks or months pushing that desire but pretty soon, you'll be heading down the hill and having to run to catch up. Determine in your mind you're going to do what it takes to get your husband and you on that path. As you give him one experience today with visuals, surprise, compliments, and excitement that fuels his imagination and desire for the next time. Just like any other muscle the more you use it the easier it becomes. Do not lose heart. There are many ways you can enjoy your husband. Be bold. Realize he is going through a lot and give him a lot of grace to not take it personally. Push through the difficulty and keep your vision on a fulfilling and fiery passionate marriage.

Your Support

Realize that a man with normal testosterone levels tends to have a normal libido, aka sex drive. That means he likes sex, he craves sex, and hopefully he has regular mutually satisfying sex with his wife. If he is not meeting that norm, there are things that need to be addressed. It may be helpful to consider him sick and needing care. If you think of your husband as needing to be 'nursed to health', the pain of rejection and disinterest may be easier not to take personally. He is not operating as a healthy man should (and a man following God's word should). So, as the sensual, confident wife you may have to do extra work to get him 'better'. Of course any of the problems listed here can have a powerful impact on his sex drive. What can you do while working on the other areas? You can encourage him. You can be his cheerleader. You can continue to remind him that you *want* him as you're helping him in other areas.

Steamy To-Do:

Plan and execute an extra heated evening for him. Try a desire technique you never have before, ie: chair dance, lap dance or strip tease. All this before giving him a wonderful oral experience.

Vision for 30 Years of Passion

Notes From Ms. Susan:

What keeps you confident that you'll make it for the next 40+ years?

Honestly that the last 5 years have been better than the first five. I mean it just keeps getting better. And I am finding out now that there is this sweet period in your life where there's actually significantly less stress in your life and in your marriage than there ever has been with maybe the exception of the early days.

In our case, our parents are very independent still. Our children are very independent and in a good place. So we don't have internal stressors. I mean there are stresses in our jobs and there might be stresses in our friends' lives and things like that. At the moment we're in this incredibly nice place where you really can just settle into it.

In this moment we have the depth of love that we didn't have when we were very young. And now we have the time to spend with each other that we did have when we were very young. So it's really great. It actually feels like it is going to be better having the next 30 years together!

Rely On Jesus

What a vision of marriage! This is my prayer for you, dear reader. That you would spend these days, weeks, and months investing in the delight of your husband for the benefit of your entire life and eternal rewards. That you would enjoy thirty years of fun-filled nights and giggling mornings and then enjoy another even better thirty. That through your marriage, God would fulfill His plans in your life. I want to encourage you that even with the best love life, the best sex-schedule, the best lovemaking attitude, you will still need Jesus at the center of your heart and in the middle of your marriage. He wants you so much more than you can ever imagine. He wants you to come to Him and share your worries, your cares, your marriage, and your intimacy.

May your marriage be a place of wholeness and support to run "with perseverance the race marked out for us" (Heb 12:1).

Write in your Workbook #53. Look back at the goal you made in the very beginning. Have you a greater vision for your marriage now? Update that goal and write a final prayer to the Lord asking him to guide you in making your goal a reality.

Pray with me: *Father, I thank you for this journey of understanding my marriage and how you made me and my husband. I ask that you would guide me in living this out. Help me to truly love my husband. Lord, in all, I commit my marriage to you and believe you will do things that I cannot do. I ask you for the grace and strength to truly love and serve him, keeping no record of wrongs. I love you and invite you to walk out this journey with me.*

Thank You

Thank you ladies for this journey. I believe as you actively love your husband you'll be surprised at the amazing things God will do in your life! I hope this has been inspiring and empowering for you. I would love to hear from you and learn what God is doing in you and your marriage: belah@delightyourmarriage.com.

Share Honestly

Beloved reader, please consider who else in your life would benefit from this material. Truly if it has affected your life, others need to hear. I ask that you would send them the link: www.delightyourmarriage.com/resources and allow them to get the material online. If you bought an ebook, I ask that you would not send it without their purchase.

Coaching with Belah!

If this material has impacted to you but you need to go deeper, I would love to coach you one on one. So, often generalities can move us quite a lot but more personally tailored advising is what will make the most significant difference. You can reach me at belah@delightyourmarriage.com. I am happy to discuss via email your concerns and discuss whether coaching is the right next step for your situation.

Thank you so much for reading. I hope and pray that this has been a life-supporting and encouraging journey for you.

God bless you, your family and your marriage.

Delight Your Husband
Work Cited

Section II Love The Act

1. Yen, Hope. "Census: Divorces Decline In United States." *Huff Post Divorce*. Huffington Post, 18 May 2011. Web. 13 May 2014. <http://www.huffingtonpost.com/2011/05/18/census-divorces-decline-i_n_863639.html>.
2. Jaffe, Esq., Wendy. "Top 10 Reasons Marriages Fail." *Divorce.com*. 1 Jan. 2013. Web. 11 May 2014. <http://divorce.com/top-10-reasons-marriages-fail/>.
3. Kerner, PhD, Ian. "Sex or Money: What Makes You Happier?" *CNN Health*. CNN.com, 12 Oct. 2012. Web. 11 May 2014. <http://www.cnn.com/2012/10/04/health/kerner-sex-money/>.
4. Fisch, MD, Harry, and Karen Moline. "Erection, Interrupted." *The New Naked*. Naperville: Sourcebooks, 2014. 93-95. Print.
5. Driscoll, Mark, and Grace Driscoll. "Sex: God, Gross, or Gift." *Real Marriage*. Nashville: Thomas Nelson, 2012. 113. Print.
6. Dillow, Linda, and Lorraine Pintus. "What's Not Okay In Bed?" *Intimate Issues*. Colorado Springs: WaterBrook, 1999. 199-201. Print.
7. Dillow, Joseph. *Solomon on Sex*. Thomas Nelson, 1977. 27. Print.
8. Driscoll, Mark, and Grace Driscoll. "Can We____." *Real Marriage*. Nashville: Thomas Nelson, 2012. 186. Print.
9. Keller, Timothy. "Sex and Marriage." *Meaning of Marriage*. New York: Penguin Group, 2011. 220. Print.
10. Penner, Clifford L. *Gift of Sex*. Nashville: Thomas Nelson, 2003. Print.

Section III Love Yourself

1. Brown, Brene, PhD LMSW. *Daring Greatly*. New York: Penguin Group, 2012. Print.

2. "Fatality Analysis Reporting System (FARS) Encyclopedia." *NCSA Data Resource Website*. NHTSA, 1 Jan. 2013. Web. 13 May 2014. <http://www-fars.nhtsa.dot.gov/Main/index.aspx>.

3. Driscoll, Mark. *Sex: God, Gross, or Gift? Real Marriage #6 Sermon Notes*. Mars Hill Church, 22 Feb. 2012. Web. 15 May 2014. <https://marshill.com/2012/02/22/sex-god-gross-or-gift-real-marriage-6-sermon-notes>.

4. Cass, PhD, Vivienne. *The Elusive Orgasm*. Cambridge: Da Capo, 2007. Print.

5. Kerner, PhD, Ian. "The Tongue Is Mightier Than The Sword." *She Comes First*. New York: HarperCollins, 2004. 29-31. Print.

6. Rosenau, Douglas. "Making Love to Your Wife." *A Celebration of Sex*. Nashville: Thomas Nelson, 2002. 153-54. Print.

Section IV Love Your Husband

1. Kerner, PhD, Ian. "Getting a 'Head-Heart' on Great Sex." *He Comes Next*. New York: e-HarperCollins, 2006. 285-86 of 442. Kindle File.

2. Fisch, MD, Harry, and Karen Moline. "Introduction." *The New Naked*. Naperville: Sourcebooks, 2014. xii-xiv. Print.

3. Covey, Stephen. "Seek First to Understand, Then to Be Understood." *Seven Habits of Highly Effective People*. New York: Simon & Schuster, 1989.

4. Rosenau, Douglas. "Making Love to Your Wife." *A Celebration of Sex*. Nashville: Thomas Nelson, 2002. 154. Print.

Section V Love His Member

1. Fisch, MD, Harry, and Karen Moline. "Satisfaction." *The New Naked*. Naperville: Sourcebooks, 2014. 8. Print.

2. Fisch, MD, Harry, and Karen Moline. "Erection, Interrupted." *The New Naked*. Naperville: Sourcebooks, 2014. 78. Print.

3. Kerner, PhD, Ian. "Male Sexual Response." *He Comes Next*. New York: e-HarperCollins, 2006. 104-106 of 442. Kindle File.

4. Kerner, PhD, Ian. "The Male Brain." *He Comes Next*. New York: e-HarperCollins, 2006. **169 of 442**. Kindle File.

5. Fisch, MD, Harry, and Karen Moline. "Satisfaction." *The New Naked*. Naperville: Sourcebooks, 2014. 9. Print.

6. New York, I Love You. Perf. Robin Wright and Chris Cooper. Vivendi Entertainment, 2008. DVD.

7. Kerner, PhD, Ian. "Fillin' Good." *He Comes Next*. New York: e-HarperCollins, 2006. **350 of 442**. Kindle File.

8. Kerner, PhD, Ian. "Arousal, Part 1." *He Comes Next*. New York: e-HarperCollins, 2006. **318-20 of 442**. Kindle File.

9. Kerner, PhD, Ian. "Male Sexual Response." *He Comes Next*. New York: e-HarperCollins, 2006. **128-29 of 442**. Kindle File.

10. Kerner, PhD, Ian. "Sex or Money: What Makes You Happier?" *CNN Health*. CNN.com, 12 Oct. 2012. Web. 11 May 2014. <http://www.cnn.com/2012/10/04/health/kerner-sex-money/>.

11. Bassil, Nazem. "The Benefits and Risks of Testosterone Replacement Therapy: A Review."*US National Library of Medicine National Institutes of Health*. NCBI, 22 Jan. 2009. Web. 11 July 2014. <http://www.ncbi.nlm.nih.gov/pmc/articles/PMC2701485/>.

12. Derrer, MD, David. "How Low Testosterone Affects Health, Mood and Sex." WebMD, 5 Oct. 2014. Web. 16 Oct. 2014. <http://www.webmd.com/sex-relationships/low-testosterone-8/treatment>.

13. Harding, Anne. "Erectile Dysfunction? Try Losing Weight." *CNN Health*. CNN.com, 5 Aug. 2011. Web. 15 June 2014. <http://www.cnn.com/2011/HEALTH/08/05/erectile.dysfunction.lose.weight/>.

14. Fisch, MD, Harry, and Karen Moline. "Satisfaction." *The New Naked*. Naperville: Sourcebooks, 2014. 40. Print.

Made in the USA
Coppell, TX
15 June 2021